To Fletcher, with
best regards,

Wes

ENVIRONMENTAL CONSULTATION

ENVIRONMENTAL CONSULTATION

by

C. Wesley Morse

PRAEGER SPECIAL STUDIES • PRAEGER SCIENTIFIC

New York • Philadelphia • Eastbourne, UK
Toronto • Hong Kong • Tokyo • Sydney

Library of Congress Cataloging in Publication Data

Morse, C. Wesley.
  Environmental consultation.

  Includes index.
  1. Environmental law—United States. 2. Environmental
mediation—United States. 3. Environmental law. 4. Environmental mediation. I. Title.
KF3775.M68 1984   344.73′046   83-24802
ISBN 0-03-064246-9 (alk. paper) 347.30446
ISBN 0-03-064247-7 (pbk. : alk. paper)

Published in 1984 by Praeger Publishers
CBS Educational and Professional Publishing
a Division of CBS Inc.
521 Fifth Avenue, New York, NY 10175 USA
© 1984 by Praeger Publishers

456789 052 987654321

Printed in the United States of America
on acid-free paper

To Dede

Acknowledgments

Many people have contributed advice and encouragement to the preparation of this book. I am grateful to all of them. However, I would particularly like to express my appreciation to the following: George Steiner of UCLA for his thoughtful review of my ideas in the early stages; Dean Mohamed Moustafa of the School of Business Administration, California State University, Long Beach; and Professor T. Kempner, principal, Henley, the Management College, Oxfordshire, England, for the provision of time and services to work on this manuscript; as well as my colleagues, Ron Edwards, Keith MacMillan, and Bernard Taylor at Henley for their comments and suggestions after reviewing portions of the manuscript. I would also like to thank my able research assistants, Carla Beam in California and Adrian Campbell at Henley in England, as well as those responsible for the laborious job of typing and editing the manuscript: my wife, Dede, for editing and typing early drafts and Mary Nelson for the final manuscript typing. Without the capable, and above all, cheerful cooperation of all these people, I would not have completed this book.

Contents

I found him in the shining
of the stars
I mark'd him in the flowers
of his fields—
But in his way with men
I find him not

Tennyson

Introduction

At the end of 1980, a distinguished group of business leaders, government regulators, and environmentalists met at Stanford University to explore the problems inherent in protecting our natural environment during the 1980s. This was the Symposium on Corporate Environmental Decision Making. During several days of formal and informal talks, an important theme persistently emerged: the current adversarial process of environmental regulation is not working.

Speaker after speaker presented differing views of this same phenomenon: "While there is agreement on environmental goals, our efforts to achieve them at reasonable cost are being frustrated by the regulation process itself." In the words of Michele Corash, then general counsel of the U.S. Environmental Protection Agency, "Corporate decisions on the substance of environmental problems have been replaced by decisions about how to play the adversarial game. I don't think any of us has benefited as a result."[1]

Though several years have passed, we are little nearer today to the solution of a debilitating deadlock between government and industry than we were at that meeting.

Consider for a moment the problems faced by the Northern Tier Pipeline Company, a consortium headed by U.S. Steel Pipeline Corporation. When this firm tried to build a $1.9 billion conduit to carry Alaskan oil from Port Angeles, Washington, to Clearbrook, Minnesota, it was required to obtain 1,500 permits and environmental clearances. Though the process was started in 1976, by 1982 it still had not received clearance from the state of Washington to build a needed ship terminal in Port Angeles. In the end, the port construction was denied by the state on environmental grounds. During that long six-year period, a fierce political battle had raged over the jobs-versus-environment issues of the project. The community was divided and the company poured millions of dollars into a project that was destined never to materialize.

Industry-government confrontations that produce results of this kind have come to be accepted as likely when business considers major projects. Yet, harmful as this is, Ronald Fox, professor at Harvard, points out that the same hostility and paralysis exists across the full range of regulatory contacts.

Today, most of the dealings between business and government are adversarial, as government probes, inspects,

> taxes, influences, regulates, and punishes. . . . Business
> managers at all levels negotiate delays, defend themselves
> in lawsuits, and otherwise seek to minimize the impact of
> government on their operations.[2]

I have written this book because I am deeply concerned about the harm being done to both industry and the environment by the philosophy behind our regulatory system — and because I know there is an alternative that will work much better. That alternative can almost be summed up in one word: consultation.

In fact, the process of consultation between environmental stakeholders is so widely used in the rest of the industrial world that the United States literally stands alone in its choice of administrative policy.

The Northern Tier outcome, for example, could not have happened in most other industrial countries. The consultative process employed in environmental affairs would have persuaded the firm at the start that the project would not be successful the way it was designed. Planners would then have had an opportunity to select a more favorable location for the ship terminal, and the pipeline might now be operational. Yet, in the United States, courts have consistently ruled that to consult with government agencies during the planning stages of such a project could violate the fairness provisions of the U.S. Administrative Procedures Act. The firm must develop its plans based on its own assumptions about environmental law before applying for approval by government.

More harmful yet, the Environmental Protection Agency (EPA) and other regulation makers are usually prohibited from discussing proposed regulations with any interested party during their development. Thus, government is often denied the latest and best technical knowledge as well as the point of view of both industry and environmentalists during the vital regulation gestation period. It is not surprising that regulations resulting from this system are often unrealistic and unnecessarily costly.

For example, in December 1978, the Environmental Protection Agency proposed its long awaited hazardous waste regulations. This was a new area for the EPA, mandated by Congress, involving complex new technology and affecting hundreds of industries. Literature and expertise in the field were notably scarce.

Following publication of its draft regulations, EPA received a seven-foot high stack of questions and comments. It had from July 1979 until May 1980 to evaluate these and issue the new regulations. During this entire period, the EPA staff was barred from discussions with anyone employed in the affected industries, thus eliminating the most extensive source of technical information in this esoteric field. To have contacted industry could have caused the courts to invalidate the regulations under the ex parte rule for conflict of interest.

These examples highlight but two aspects of a rigid, distrustful, adversarial process, mandated by our laws, which should be replaced by a consultative system designed to meet the special environmental and political needs of this country. How environmental consultation can come about is a story to be told in some detail in the following pages. That it is possible is quite certain. Having studied the systems of consultation used by every other Western industrial country, I know that they work. Some systems, of course, work better than others. Some utilize elements of consultation that are more suited to our society than others. It has been my job to sort these systems out and to tell my readers about them — more than that, to make specific workable recommendations for the inclusion of consultation in U.S. environmental regulation.

This book begins with a review of the history of the rise of environmental consciousness during the decade and a half beginning in 1965. That story constitutes Part I of the book. It is an important section because if we understand the nature of the public commitment to environmental values, we can infer a great deal about what the process of consultation in this country must include. It must, for example, recognize the place that environmental values occupy in our national priorities and the role of environmental activists in maintaining that place.

Part II looks at the costs and benefits of a clean environment, examines how we are trying to achieve our goals, and analyzes some of the problems we are encountering. In this section the reader will find the results of my studies comparing U.S. environmental regulation with that of other industrial countries. The benefits of environmental consultation are discussed, and several promising approaches to consultation in the United States that are going on now are described.

The last chapter of Part II brings together the data and insights of the previous discussions to focus on some specific aspects of environmental consultation in the United States. It answers several questions that are asked throughout the book. How can we stimulate creativity to benefit the environment? What ends are served by advance discussion of proposed regulations? How can consultation work in a political system that values freedom of information? What role should environmentalists play in a U.S. consultative process? Can processes that work in other countries be used here? The answers to these and other questions provide a framework for the environmental consultation proposal, introduced in this chapter. Such a process could be used to institute specific consultative structure and process in our regulatory system.

In Part III we will consider, through the use of case studies, the process of environmental regulation as it has been applied to a large chemical processing plant in the United States and as it affects the coal strip mining industry in Britain. We thus have an opportunity to compare the delicate but decisive role of consultation in the operation of British industry with the adversarial command-and-control philosophy of the U.S. approach.

People in the United States generally agree on our environmental goals. Business managers, like other citizens, understand the need for clean air and water and the protection of our natural heritage. Too many have made the mistake, however, of assuming that the existing regulatory system is the only way of delivering these benefits. My interviews with managers indicate that what business opposes most is our system of controls, which refuses to concede the right of participation to any but the Congress and a handful of regulators.

During the research for this book, I talked to scores of managers who are so disheartened by our present regulatory approach that they are beginning to doubt that reaching environmental goals is possible at all. Others, stung by the command nature of the system, have resorted to evasion and distortion to avoid dealing with regulations whenever possible. Far from enlisting the support and challenging the creativity of U.S. managers, our laws are driving them outside the system. Other countries have learned to use the talents of business and other stakeholders to protect the environment. Must we spurn these resources? I don't think so. The know-how and ingenuity of the U.S. business system has always been one of our strongest national resources. I believe that, through a policy of consultation, that resource can be enlisted to achieve our environmental as well as our economic goals. This book tells how it can be done.

NOTES

1. Michele B. Corash, "Government Regulation: A Consensual Alternative," in Proceedings of the Symposium on Corporate Environmental Decision Making, Stanford University, November 1980.

2. Ronald J. Fox, "Breaking the Regulatory Deadlock," Harvard Business Review 59 (September-October 1981):97.

PART I
THE RISE OF ENVIRONMENTAL CONSCIOUSNESS

1
Environmental Roots

It was Earth Day, April 22, 1970. Even after the lapse of intervening years, one is left gasping a little when attempting to describe it. The sheer power of the concept — a day dedicated to the preservation of our planet — seemed enough to unite Americans. But there must have been more to it than just that simple concept. Cynical as we are, how could millions of citizens be induced to suspend their daily enterprises long enough to participate in so ecumenical a celebration? A little further on I hope to supply an answer to that question, but first we will look at that day — what it was and how it came about. Support for Earth Day cut across politics and ideologies in a way we had never seen in the peacetime history of this country. For here, in microcosm, was that extremely rare event — the feelings and attitudes of an entire nation condensed in time and neatly displayed for us to see. The statistics relating to Earth Day are indeed impressive:

- 20 million people were estimated to have participated, half of them school children.
- Several cities (according to the <u>New York Times</u>) held celebrations involving from 100,000 to 250,000 people.
- Special programs were held at 2,000 colleges, 10,000 high schools, and in virtually every town in the country.

Beyond this sketchy data, there is a record of organization and performance that provides an even better insight into the unique character of Earth Day. Senator Gaylord Nelson, Democrat of Wisconsin, is said to have been the first to propose a celebration of the earth. The idea was born while the senator was attending a conference in Santa Barbara in 1969, which was concerned with the tragic oil spill in the Pacific Ocean margins of that city six months earlier. He had been impressed with the Vietnam "teach-ins" of a few years prior, which had been held on many university campuses. He reasoned that a similar activity might be a useful way to draw attention to the pollution problems then becoming such a national issue. A nationwide teach-in could provide publicity for issues he was concerned about and at the same time could impart useful learning to those who chose to participate. The scheme was to succeed well beyond the expectations that the senator expressed at the time.

He announced a plan, cosponsored by Representative Pete McCloskey, a California Republican, in Seattle on September 20, 1969. A staff of young men and women was assembled, and publicity work for Earth Day began, with financial help from the federal government, foundations, and industry. The timing was perfect for the organizers' purposes. Public opinion was running strongly in favor of protecting our air and water from pollution. For example, a Gallup poll conducted in April 1970 (admittedly with results influenced somewhat by Earth Day itself) indicated that 53 percent of those questioned considered that reducing pollution of air and water should be the first order of priority for the national government.[1] In 1965 Gallup had found that only 17 percent of U.S. citizens held such an opinion.[2]

Another measure of the public support for Earth Day came from Washington, D.C., where politicians were aware of the impact of the pollution issues involved. Senators and Congress members of both parties, as well as members of President Nixon's cabinet, took advantage of the occasion to take to the stump at teach-ins and similar functions across the nation. "Everyone I've talked to is making a speech somewhere," said Representative Pete McCloskey.[3] News reporters were to find: Senator Gaylord Nelson, predictably, jumping from the University of Wisconsin to Denver and then to Berkeley, California, for additional speeches; Senator Edward M. Kennedy was at Yale; Barry Goldwater was at Adelphi University in Garden City, New York; Clifford Case was at Princeton; Ralph W. Yarborough was at Rice University in Houston; and Edmund S. Muskie was at the University of Pennsylvania. Dozens of other senators and Congress members fanned out across the country.

Most departments of the federal government provided special programs such as films or lectures about their special interests in relation to the control of pollution. For example, the Agriculture Department provided a program of speeches and films focusing on the earth "unspoiled and despoiled," while cabinet officers were making speeches in much the same way as our elected representatives.

Most cities provided both time and space for celebration of the day, and in most places it was seen by participants as a celebration. New York City gives us an example of the kind of activities that went on, and as cities went, it was by no means unusual. Fifth Avenue between Fourteenth and Fifty-ninth Streets was closed to traffic for two hours, providing a giant mall for the congregation of pedestrians. Fourteenth Street from Third to Seventh Avenues was closed to traffic from noon to midnight, supplying an area for booths operated by various organizations with a viewpoint about ecology.

Union Square, the focus of dozens of activities, was a popular option for the crowds. According to the New York Times: "At any given time there were probably 20,000 people in the square, but the crowds were constantly on the move, so it was likely that many more than 100,000 passed through the square in the course of the day."[4] There were hundreds of options for activities that people could take part in. On Seventeenth Street, thousands crowded into a polyethlene bubble to "breathe clean, filtered air."

Everywhere, one felt a spirit of goodwill and cooperation. It seemed as though government, industry, and public interest groups were vying to show who was the most enthusiastic. The New York Times, again describing the holiday mood of the occasion, says it was exemplified by "members of the architectural firm of Warner, Burns, Toan & Lunde, who spread a yellow-and-white quilt on the asphalt near Fifty-seventh Street, put a tulip in a wine bottle for a center piece and enjoyed a picnic in the sun. A laughing crowd gathered around them and sang 'Happy Earth Day to You.'"[5]

More touching perhaps than the cavorting high spirits of adults were the deeds of small children. Across the nation, schoolchildren, Boy Scouts, Girl Scouts, and children from ghettos and affluent suburbs tackled projects aimed to demonstrate their concern for the environment. Trees were planted in record numbers, parks were cleaned up, and small groups picnicked and enjoyed the outdoors with zest.

On college campuses and at high schools, the teach-ins consisted of learning about the earth and the environmental processes that maintain it. There were speeches, but the day was not designed for politics. Most participants felt a kind of dedication and a desire for a continuing involvement in the preservation of our environment.

Rene Dubos had expressed concern earlier that year about how long these feelings would last. In February he had told an audience at Barnard College "direct action programs on specific limited issues will not keep the movement [to protect the environment] going." He said that such programs as Earth Day would "soon engender boredom and lassitude." "Even you here," he said to the students, "will forget about them when you become Vice-President of the local bank, as many of you will."[6] He went on to suggest that long-term goals of the quality of life and lower economic growth should be pursued.

On April 24, mindful of Dubos's comments, the youthful staff of Environmental Action Inc., the promoters of Earth Day, announced it would remain in operation as a coordinating agency for ecological groups. The national coordinator of the group, Denis Hays, said the organization would drop its tax-free status so that it could continue as a force to lobby, litigate, and engage in other political activity on behalf of the environment.

In summing up, Senator Gaylord Nelson said:

> You can be sure there will never be another political campaign like the one in 1968, when not one of the three candidates for President considered the environment an issue worthy of a major speech. It is nothing short of remarkable how rapidly the issue has been thrust into the politics, the conversation, and the literature of the country . . . we have witnessed unprecedented accomplishments in public environmental awareness and in the areas of political and legal activities, such as the growth of public interest environmental law firms. . . . They must be measured as beginnings, as we pose the question: "Do we have to destroy tomorrow in order to live today?" The answer to that question must be no.[7]

As Earth Day had demonstrated, the concern of citizens for the natural environment seemed to burst upon the public scene like some gigantic wave, engulfing lesser values and institutions, rendering objections impotent, or at the very least querulous in character. In 1970 it would have been difficult for the most obtuse curmudgeon to have said or have heard a word against what seemed to most of us the wave of the future. However, if serious study of the future had been sufficiently advanced in earlier periods, say the 1950s, someone would surely have predicted the rise of environmental consciousness in the period between 1965 and 1980. The convergence of social trends so prized as indicators by futurists would certainly have pointed to the massive concern that people at almost every station in society were to exhibit for environmental issues.

Consider for a moment the factors brewing in society that would provide a cornucopia of needs and pressures, pushing the public into a wider acceptance of environmental protection from about 1965 on.

First, it seems that we stood at the crossroads of the continuation of a fairly rich history of conservation (which is best expressed in our national park system) and an unprecedented affluence that provided more people than ever with the leisure time and the opportunity to enjoy the outdoor resources of our country. These resources were, in fact, in short supply by the early 1960s. This fostered concerns about whether our children, let alone ourselves, would be able to enjoy the beauty of this country's outdoors as we had in the past.

I recall my own shock and disbelief when in 1960 my young son and I shouldered packs for an outing in California's Sierra Nevada Mountains. What had been wilderness country in my own comparatively recent youth was by then overcrowded with hikers, campers, and even motorcycle riders — all competing for the same small remote valley where I once fished in isolation. Mine was a feeling shared by many other Americans that year.

Second, by the early 1960s science had been pointing for some time to the fact that everywhere on earth we were depleting our natural resources of every kind at a rapid and even reckless pace. Studies were even suggesting that the precious resource of an atmosphere at livable temperatures was being destroyed by a "greenhouse effect" caused by the collection of industrially produced hydrocarbons and particulates high in the atmosphere, which could trap heat radiating out of space and raise the temperature of the biosphere to a point that would be intolerable to human life.

Third, the world population was increasing at an exponential rate, reviving Malthusian visions of widespread starvation and disease within the span of a few generations.

Fourth, we were awakening to the degree to which our air and water were polluted by pesticides, smog, and industrial contaminants.

Fifth, and possibly last, there was a disaffection with the norms of established values on the part of many young people. This was generated from a variety of sources, not the least of which was the Vietnam War. It led to a desire for an alternate lifestyle on the part of a very large segment of the college-age population. Many of these concerns were to be subsumed under the title of "quality of life," but that came later on.

While the conservation and in turn the environmental movement in the United States owes a great deal to the ideals of the Progressive Era, which had its political roots near the end of the nineteenth century, it is important to remember that the intellectual forebearers of conservation were respectable at an even earlier date. Thus, Henry David Thoreau is quoted as saying, in the 1840s, "What's the use of a house if you haven't got a tolerable planet to put it on?"

Westward expansion and development of the wilderness for the benefit of settlers, following the Civil War, provided little sympathy for environmental values, and hence really important national recognition of the need to protect the environment was to wait until later in the century. John Muir was the catalyst of conservation energies during the later years of the nineteenth century, and he found allies in two U.S. presidents, both associated with the Progressive Era. Grover Cleveland and Theodore Roosevelt were jointly responsible for focusing public interest on the need for conservation of our wilderness. Thus, the Forest Reserve Act of 1891 (forest reserves were later to become national forests) and the designation of Yosemite and Sequoia in 1890 as national parks were significant steps in the forging of conservation values. Muir was to be instrumental in influencing Theodore Roosevelt to make the protection of the wilderness a rather important part of his personal and political philosophy. In one of the most significant presidential acts on behalf of conservation, Roosevelt in 1908 called a conference of governors of all the states to propose a policy of "protection, preservation, and wise-use" of natural resources.[8]

Two elements of the concern for conservation were to affect the contemporary environmental movement, each in its own way. First, as has been indicated, the growth of these concerns provided a base for the development of later, stronger values. In addition to this, there existed as today an element of opposition to conservation, centered at the time mainly in the western states. Colorado was an example of a state's preference for attracting new settlers and developing industry rather than preserving the natural environment. Angry settlers charged federal violation of both personal and states' rights, proclaiming the prerogative to develop and settle "where they pleased." Conservationists soon learned that the federal government and eastern legislators were more sympathetic to their cause than were those actually on the land. Out of the alliance thus forged came the principle (now established in our national conscience and of incalculable importance to modern environmentalists) that the federal government has a right to set aside or control lands where there is a consensus that development might operate "to the detriment of all the people." Thus, historian G. M. McCarthy notes that the federal government adopted the philosophy that "if the forests and waters and mineral wealth of the west were to be saved for the use of future generations, it would have to be done through federal regulation. The fact that western states like Colorado never agreed formed the crux of the conservation furor for the next two decades."[9]

While there were sporadic efforts to extend and consolidate the conservation programs of that period, for example, Civilian Conservation Corps under the New Deal and additional National Parks initiated by many administrations, no really new directions evolved in conservation until the 1960s. It is important to remember, however, that the social value of conservation was firmly established by the end of the first decade of this century. Institutions like the Sierra Club (founded by John Muir) and the Audubon Society kept the interest of the public and various legislative bodies alive over the years. In the 1960s, when our outdoor and wilderness resources became in short supply relative to the growing demand for outdoor recreation, there was a clear and vibrant social concern for the priority of conservation and all that had come to imply, including a clean natural environment.

Concerns of the period about the depletion of our natural resources were reflective of trends in scientific knowledge that had again been gathering for a number of years. The argument advanced by Harvey Wheeler in his <u>Saturday Review</u> article in March 1970 represents the kind of thinking that was making sense to a lot of people at the time.

> . . . but the essence of the real problem is what Kenneth Watt calls the ecocidal asymptote. It is to the new politics of ecology what $E=mc^2$ was to the thermonuclear era.
>
> The ecocidal asymptote runs as follows: Statistical studies of the pattern of exploitation of every natural resource can be plotted as two curves. One represents the rate of depletion of a resources, the other represents the technological capacity for its exploitation. Both curves are exponential; that is, in the beginning they rise very gradually. But their rate of increase is always rising, pushing their curves up ever more steeply until they reach a vertical explosion. Both follow the same pattern at the same rate, exploding, asymptotically, at the same time.
>
> As an illustration, consider the ocean's fisheries — the blue whale, the salmon, the tuna. In the beginning, the supply is virtually unlimited, and harvesting techniques make little or no dent in the available supply. Soon fishing techniques improve. As this situation becomes apparent, it spurs on competition to get more and more while the getting is good. Ever more efficient fishing techniques are invented, and their rate of efficiency rises in direct ratio to the depletion of the resource until the point arrives when the ultimate in fishing technology coincides with the extinction of the species. This "falling together" of the technology and resource depletion curves is the ecocidal asymptote. It is the inimical process that characterizes our age, the enemy of the new politics of ecology. The death of one resource leads to the depletion of another; one technological fix begets another. Each of our ecocidal crises is interconnected with all the others, and none can be solved in isolation.[10]

Thus, the principal concern about the depletion of resources was, and is, not so much the admittedly important fact of depletion, but the effect of rapidly rising rates of depletion. The exponential relationship describing the latter stages of shortages can be frightening indeed. One need only look at the steeply escalating price relationships in the oil industry between 1973 and 1981, when demand remained strong, to sense the havoc inherent in this stage of relative shortage. The prospect of several resources reaching this situation at once has been rightly described by Wheeler and others as one that could overwhelm the world economy on a scale never seen before.

Paul Ehrlich, the Stanford biologist, was to rivet the public attention on the problems of growing population with the publication of his book _The Population Bomb_ in 1968. Concern about overpopulation and its potential relationship to the resource problem was a continuing thread woven through environmental policy issues throughout the 1970s. The impact of Ehrlich's ideas looms large in the "single child family" ethic still pervading our value system. His book has been responsible in large part for the resulting lower rates of population growth during the last 15 years.

The issue that was to have the greatest impact on public policy in the long run, and that is of central importance to this book, is pollution. Certainly no one contributed more to public understanding of the pollution problems caused by years of environmental neglect and rapid acceleration of chemical technology than Rachel Carson.

At the peak of her career, Carson, trained in genetics, was editor in chief of the U.S. Wildlife Service's publications. She was a fine writer, having authored the best-selling _The Sea Around Us_ in 1951. During the 1950s she became very concerned about the effects of persistently using pesticides such as DDT. In her book, _Silent Spring_,[11] published in 1962, she wrote forcefully, citing considerable evidence of the concentration of DDT in higher members of the food chain. She was able to document correlations between these concentrations and the decline in populations of several bird species. The book was first published in a serial version in the _New Yorker_ in 1961, and it attracted widespread attention. The metaphor of a "silent spring" referred to the likelihood of an environment so poisoned that spring would be without the familiar sounds of birds and insects.

Rachel Carson's arguments are generally credited with inducing the President's Scientific Advisory Committee to appoint a pesticide study panel to investigate her charges. In 1963 the panel recommended "orderly reduction in the use of pesticides."

Pollution, including but by no means limited to uncontrolled use of pesticides, as we have already seen, was to become the high-priority issue of the environmental movement in the years that followed. Here at the junction of the issues of conservation, public health, and resource shortage was a problem that everyone was concerned with to one degree or another. Time was to show that a clean environment was an objective that just about everyone could agree on, at least in principle.

It is probably not necessary to dwell on the fifth and last factor that contributed importantly to the development of environmental concerns between 1965 and 1980. This was the enormously energetic manner in which many young people of the period rebelled against the establishment's values. The phenomenon was such a dominant, and controversial, part of the public scene that no one can have escaped forming a set of opinions about it. It certainly contributed in many ways to the development of environmental values. However, the countervalues involved changed so many other relationships as well that it is difficult in this space to analyze the resulting complex network of influence on U.S. society.[12] I will thus be content to leave readers with the assertion that the emergence of counterculture values strongly influenced our environmental concerns.

This chapter has attempted to show that long-term pressures on technological and social values in the United States have produced a predictable result. That result is a concern for the environment in which we live, which stands very high among our national priorities. This issue of priorities will be important to the further analysis of national environmental policy. Later chapters will deal with the effects of this environmental consensus on legislation and regulation, as well as its proper role in the determination of public policy.

NOTES

1. _The Gallup Poll: Public Opinion 1935-1971_ (New York: Random House, 1972), p. 2248.
2. Ibid., p. 1939.
3. _New York Times,_ April 23, 1970, p. 30.
4. Ibid.
5. Ibid.
6. _New York Times,_ February 1, 1970, p. 55.
7. Quoted in Odom Fanning, _Man and His Environment: Citizen Action_ (New York: Harper & Row, 1975), p. 34.
8. G. M. McCarthy, "Retreat from Responsibility: The Colorado Legislature in the Conservation Era, 1876-1908," _Rocky Mountain Social Science_ 10 (April 1973):27-36.
9. Ibid.
10. Harvey Wheeler, "The Politics of Ecology," _Saturday Review_, March 7, 1970, p. 52.
11. Rachel Carson, _Silent Spring_ (New York: Houghton Mifflin, 1962).

12. For a discussion of changing values and the phenomena of the 1960s by a group of distinguished authors, see Kurt Baier and Nicholas Rescher, eds., <u>Values and the Future,</u> (New York: Free Press, 1969). Also see Eli Ginsberg, <u>Values and Ideals of American Youth</u> (New York: Columbia University Press, 1961).

2
People and Ideas

An interesting aspect about the rise of environmental interest in the United States is the extent to which its ideas were rooted in the established academic and scientific communities. Perhaps the respectability that environmentalism was to ultimately garner was in some measure due to the early intellectual base on which it stood. Environmentalism was not just another faddist counter-culture movement as was suspected by some business leaders. Though there were to be political movements of a more transient nature, concern about the environment was a fact, based on truly startling and, in fact, frightening aspects of humanity's interrelations with nature. As such, it was going to stand the test of time. These aspects had been carefully researched and presented to the public by some rather well qualified individuals. Our purpose in this chapter will be to get a feeling for the quality of work that went into these early influences and to assess their impact on the mood of the public.

It is fair to say that there is a truly vast body of literature about the environment, most of it published in the period that was decisive for environmental influence. The reader will thus be asked to forbear with my nomination of the most important of these. I have tried to select those ideas that had both scientific relevance and that influenced public opinion through publication.

CRISIS

One of the most startling characteristics of environmental problems is the summary fashion in which they seem to manifest themselves. The first writer to document the crisis nature of environmental pollution was Rachel Carson. Although <u>Silent Spring</u> was mentioned in the preceding chapter, it deserves further analysis here.

As I have said, Rachel Carson was well qualified to understand and summarize the research of the crisis of pesticide pollution of land and water that was already in an advanced stage when her book was published in 1962. The very disturbing nature of her message can be gleaned from this passage presented early in the book:

The most alarming of all man's assaults upon the environment is the contamination of air, earth, rivers, and sea with dangerous and even lethal materials. This pollution is for the most part irrecoverable; the chain of evil it initiates not only in the world that must support life but in living tissues is for the most part irreversible. In this now universal contamination of the environment, chemicals are the sinister and little-recognized partners of radiation in changing the very nature of the world — the very nature of its life. Strontium 90, released through nuclear explosions into the air, comes to earth in rain or drifts down as fallout, lodges in soil, enters into the grass or corn or wheat grown there, and in time takes up its abode in the bones of a human being, there to remain until his death. Similarly, chemicals sprayed on croplands or forests or gardens lie long in soil, entering into living organisms, passing from one to another in a chain of poisoning and death. Or they pass mysteriously by underground streams until they emerge and, through the alchemy of air and sunlight, combine into new forms that kill vegetation, sicken cattle, and work unknown harm on those who drink from once-pure wells. As Albert Schweitzer had said, "Man can hardly even recognize the devils of his own creation."[1]

The evidence she presented chiefly dealt with birds, although studies involving fish and other creatures were cited. Among the most dramatic, and precipitate, of the dangers to bird life that Carson reported was the plight of the robin.

The unsuspected relationship of the robin to DDT, via the link of earthworms, was first studied by a team of two ornithologists at Michigan State University, Professor George Wallace and doctoral candidate John Mehner. When Mehner began work for his doctorate in 1954, he had chosen to do research involving robin populations. Unsuspectingly, he had chosen to work with an endangered species (although the now common use of the term was not used at the time). The troublesome Dutch elm disease was the principal cause of the tragedy that Mehner was to discover. Spraying with DDT for Dutch elm disease began among the campus trees at Michigan State in 1954. Trees received an average dose over the next several years of two to six pounds each per year.

The robin population was little affected in 1954, but by the following spring the research team noticed that dead and dying robins were becoming common on the campus and that few birds could be observed in their usual foraging activities. Professor Wallace was prompted to observe, after a few seasons of spraying, "The campus is serving as a graveyard for most of the robins that attempt to take up residence in the spring." Wallace was deeply concerned about the reasons for the mortality, and Carson in her book takes up the train of his logic:

At first he suspected some disease of the nervous system, but soon it became evident that "in spite of the assurances of the insecticide people that their sprays were 'harmless to birds' the robins were really dying of insecticidal poisoning; they exhibited the well-known symptoms of loss of balance, followed by tremors, convulsions, and death."

Several facts suggested that the robins were being poisoned, not so much by direct contact with the insecticides as indirectly, by eating earthworms. Campus earthworms had been fed inadvertently to crayfish in a research project and all the crayfish had promptly died. A snake kept in a laboratory cage had gone into violent tremors after being fed such worms. And earthworms are the principal food of robins in the spring.

A key piece of the jigsaw puzzle of the doomed robins was soon to be supplied by Dr. Roy Barker of the Illinois Natural History Survey at Urbana. Dr. Barker's work, published in 1958, traced the intricate cycle of events by which the robins' fate is linked to the elm trees by way of the earthworms. The trees are sprayed in the spring (usually at the rate of 2 to 6 pounds of DDT per 50-foot tree, which may be the equivalent of as much as 23 pounds per acre where elms are numerous) and often again in July, at about half this concentration. Powerful sprayers direct a stream of poison to all parts of the tallest trees, killing directly not only the target organism, the bark beetle, but other insects, including pollinating species and predatory spiders and beetles. The poison forms a tenacious film over the leaves and bark. Rains do not wash it away. In the autumn the leaves fall to the ground, accumulate in sodden layers, and begin the slow process of becoming one with the soil. In this they are aided by the toil of the earthworms, who feed in the leaf litter, for elm leaves are among their favourite foods. In feeding on the leaves the worms also swallow the insecticide, accumulating and concentrating it in their bodies. Dr. Barker found deposits of DDT throughout the digestive tracts of the worms, their blood vessels, nerves, and body wall. Undoubtedly some of the earthworms themselves succumb, but others survive to become "biological magnifiers" of the poison. In the spring the robins return to provide another link in the cycle. As few as eleven large earthworms can transfer a lethal dose of DDT to a robin. And eleven worms form a small part of a day's rations to a bird that eats ten to twelve earthworms in as many minutes.

Not all robins receive a lethal dose, but another consequence may lead to the extinction of their kind as surely as fatal poisoning. The shadow of sterility lies over all the bird studies and indeed lengthens to include all living things within its potential range. There are now only two or three dozen robins to be found each spring on the entire 185-acre campus of Michigan State University, compared with a conservatively estimated 370 adults in this area before spraying. In 1954 every robin nest under observation by Mehner produced young. Towards the end of June, 1957, when at least 370 young birds (the normal replacement of the adult population) would have been foraging over the campus in the years before spraying began, Mehner could find only one young robin. A year later Dr. Wallace was to report: "At no time during the spring or summer (of 1958) did I see a fledgling robin anywhere on the main campus, and so far I have failed to find anyone else who has seen one there."

Part of this failure to produce young is due, of course, to the fact that one or more of a pair of robins dies before the nesting cycle is completed. But Wallace has significant records which point to something more sinister — the actual destruction of the birds' capacity to reproduce. He has, for example, "records of robins and other birds building nests but laying no eggs, and others laying eggs and incubating them but not hatching them. We have one record of a robin that sat on its eggs faithfully for twenty-one days and they did not hatch. The normal incubation period is thirteen days. . . . Our analyses are showing high concentrations of DDT in the testes and ovaries of breeding birds," he told a congressional committee in 1960. "Ten males had amounts ranging from 30 to 109 parts per million in the testes, and two females had 151 and 211 parts per million respectively in the egg follicles in their ovaries."

While Carson ably supported her writing with references to scientific studies such as those above, she was eloquent in her emotional appeal to public morality as well. For example, in the case of the poisoned robins, she quoted a letter from a Hinsdale, Illinois, homemaker to a leading ornithologists as follows:

> Here in our village the elm trees have been sprayed for several years (she wrote in 1958). When we moved here six years ago, there was a wealth of bird life; I put up a feeder and had a steady stream of cardinals, chickadees, downies and nuthatches all winter, and the cardinals and chickadees brought their young ones in the summer.
>
> After several years of DDT spray, the town is almost devoid of robins and starlings; chickadees have not been on my shelf for two years, and this year the cardinals are gone too; the nesting population in the neighborhood seems to consist of one dove pair and perhaps one catbird family.
>
> It is hard to explain to the children that the birds have been killed off, when they have learned in school that a Federal law protects the birds from killing or capture. "Will they ever come back?" they ask, and I do not have the answer. Is anything being done? Can anything be done? Can I do anything?*

I have already reported that Carson's work prompted the recommendation of the President's Scientific Advisory Committee that the use of DDT be curbed through legislation. Important as that step was, the impact of her work and ideas on the public and other writers was even more significant. Serialized in the _New Yorker_ magazine and surging at once to the top of the best seller list, _Silent Spring_ was to provide an important stimulus for conservation and environmental protection in general, and its impact was to last for a generation.

While Rachel Carson was documenting the scientific evidence extant about the pollution crisis in the United States, another writer, Stewart Udall, was preparing a somewhat more personal statement about crisis. In _The Quiet Crisis_ (1963), Udall strove to clarify the need for our conservation policies to be matched with the growth in affluence and population in America that threatened to overwhelm our natural resources.

> America today stands poised on a pinnacle of wealth and power, yet we live in a land of vanishing beauty, of in-

---

*From _Silent Spring_ by Rachel Carson. Copyright @ 1962 by Rachel Carson. Reprinted by permission of Houghton Mifflin Company and the estate of Rachel Carson.

creasing ugliness, of shrinking open space, and of an overall environment that is diminished daily by pollution and noise and blight. This, in brief, is the quiet conservation crisis of the 1960's.[2]

This influential book, with an introduction by John F. Kennedy, traced the history of conservation in our national conscience through the years from the early wisdom of American Indians to the early 1960s. Udall's emphasis was on the action aspects of public policy, and he strongly approved the roles of both Theodore Roosevelt and Franklin Roosevelt in contributing to the conservation movements of their times.

He called for a substantial expansion of "government leadership and government investment" in the development of solutions to conservation problems.

The book was widely quoted. It had a special appeal to young people, who were naturally concerned that their generation might not be privileged to enjoy our outdoor heritage as other groups had. While __The Quiet Crisis__ was not a scientific book, it was well balanced historically, and it helped to solidify the impression of the importance of the environment, as well as the urgency of the case for conservation.

Stanford biologist Paul Ehrlich, in 1968, raised once again the Malthusian proposition that the continued increase in population of the earth would soon outstrip the earth's ability to support that population. Though the ideas were far from new, Ehrlich introduced them in a sophisticated manner, coupling them with growing concerns about pollution and the destruction of natural resources through man-made processes. His book, __The Population Bomb__,[3] was an instant success. Both its impact on public opinion and the well-qualified scientific views it advanced warrant a further look at its premises.

Ehrlich's primary concern, as expressed in his title, was with the exponential growth of the earth's population. He was moved by more than the simple statistics of world population, grim as these were to him. He saw the result of rampant population growth being manifested in the gruesome handmaidens of starvation and disease for millions and eventually billions of people, within a relatively short period of time. His descriptions of these effects of population explosion were advanced in a rational as well as intuitively convincing way.

First, he proposed the time-honored argument dealing with the dangers of exponential population growth. His impressive advocacy of the case went as follows:

It has been estimated that the human population of 8000 B.C. was about five million people, taking perhaps one million years to get there from two and a half million.

The population did not reach 500 million until almost 10,000 years later — about 1650 A.D. This means it doubled roughly about every thousand years or so. It reached a billion people around 1850, doubling in some 200 years. It took only 80 years or so for the next doubling, as the population reached two billion around 1930. We have not completed the next doubling to four billion yet, but we now have well over three and a half billion people. The doubling time at present seems to be about 35 years. Quite a reduction in doubling times: 1,000,000 years, 1,000 years, 200 years, 80 years, 35 years. Perhaps the meaning of a doubling time of around 35 years is best brought home by a theoretical exercise. Let's examine what might happen on the absurd assumption that the population continued to double every 35 years into the indefinite future.

If growth continued at that rate for about 900 years, there would be some 60,000,000,000,000,000,000 people on the face of the earth. Sixty million billion people. This is about 100 persons for each square yard of the Earth's surface, land and sea.[4]

When Ehrlich wrote this in 1968, the world's population was 3.5 billion. As this book is being written, the Population Reference Bureau in Washington, D.C., has announced that in mid-1983 the population reached 4.7 billion.

In his calculations, Ehrlich was not unique. As I have suggested, the early framework for the logic goes all the way back to Malthus. The specific numbers were to be produced in modern times by J. H. Fremlin,[5] among others. But Ehrlich carried the analysis a step further than most other writers by including additional contemporary elements as part of the problem. He characterized the overall population problem as too many people, not enough food, and a dying planet. His concern about increasing population was thus modified and extended by his fears that we would pollute the planet, destroying its ecosystems and making a technological solution to the Malthusian problem impossible. He described the delicate balance between food and population that existed at the time The Population Bomb was first published:

In 1965-1966 mankind suffered a shocking defeat in what is now popularly called the "war on hunger." In 1966, while the population of the world increased by some 70 million people, there was no compensatory increase in food production. According to the United Nations Food and Agriculture Organization (FAO), advances in food production made in developing nations between 1955 and 1965 were wiped out by agricultural disasters in 1965 and 1966. In 1966, each person on Earth had 2% less to eat, the reduction, of course, not being uniformly distributed. Only ten countries grew more food than they consumed: the United States, Canada, Australia, Argentina, France, New Zealand, Burma, Thailand, Rumania, and South Africa. The United States produced more than half of the surplus, with Canada and Australia contributing most of the balance. All other countries, including the giants of China, India and Russia, imported more than they exported. In 1966 the United States shipped one quarter of its wheat crop, nine million tons, to India. In the process we helped change the distribution of people in the country. Thousands migrated into port cities so as to be close to the centers of wheat distribution. We also, in the opinion of some, hindered India's agricultural development. Perhaps we gave too many Indians the impression that we have unlimited capacity to ship them food. Unhappily, we do not.[6]

Ehrlich was not sanguine about the idea that a technological fix, such as implementation of the "green revolution" involving increased agricultural output, would provide answers to the population and hunger problems that he described so graphically. The vague palliative of technology had provided the shadow of hope for future generations for a long time, but Ehrlich's book contained strong denial of the effectiveness of technology alone. It was on ecological grounds that Ehrlich argued that we could not invent our way out of the problem he had propounded for us.
Here is a sample of his logic:

Our problem would be much simpler if we needed only to consider the balance between food and population. But in the long view the progressive deterioration of our environment may cause more death and misery than the food-population gap. And it is just this factor, environmental deterioration, that is almost universally ignored by those concerned with closing the food gap. . . .
Environmental changes connected with agriculture are often striking. For instance, in the United States we are paying a price for maintaining our high level of food production. Professor LaMonte Cole has written ". . . even our own young country is not immune to deterioration. We have lost many thousands of acres to erosion and gullying, and many thousand more to strip mining. It has been estimated that the agricultural value of Iowa farmland, which is about as good land as we have, is declining by 1% per year. In our irrigated lands of the West there

is the constant danger of salinization from rising water tables, while, elsewhere, from Long Island to Southern California, we have lowered water tables so greatly that in coastal regions salt water is seeping into the aquifers. Meanwhile, an estimated two thousand irrigation dams in the United States are now useless impoundments of silt, sand, and gravel."

The history of similar deterioration in other parts of the world is clear for those who know how to read it. It stretches back to the cradles of civilization in the Middle East, where in many places deserts now occupy what were once rich and productive farmlands. . . .

Plans for increasing food production, such as the Green Revolution, invariably involve large-scale efforts at environmental modification. These plans involve the "inputs" so beloved of the agricultural propagandists — especially inorganic fertilizers to enrich soils and synthetic pesticides to discourage our competitors. The new strains of wheat and rice require large amounts of fertilizer and more irrigation water than traditional ones do in order to produce their yields. Their resistance to pests is unknown; they may also need higher inputs of pesticides for protection. Growing more food also may involve the clearing of forests from additional land and the provision of irrigation water.*[7]

Ehrlich's suggestions for solutions for the population explosion were, like his description of the problem, edged with crisis. He envisaged imminent disaster if worldwide population control were not instituted within a very short time. He suggested this be done through the United Nations. He also proposed a worldwide, regionally based agricultural development system. He felt that the developed nations would have to make great sacrifices to fund these emergency programs, which could, in the end, save humanity from the apocalypse.

The most evenhanded assessment of <u>The Population Bomb</u> would give it, in retrospect, very high marks for arousing public opinion and for contributing to the change of values in the United States. While it did not accurately predict the events of the 1970s and 1980s, its contribution to the development of environmental consensus cannot be doubted.

Garrett Harden, a professor of biology at the University of California, Santa Barbara, published his influential article, "The

Tragedy of the Commons," in the journal <u>Science</u> in December 1968. The ideas of the article were among the first steps in the direction of a social theory bridging the natural environment to our social systems. The metaphor of the commons was to prove a powerful one, reintroduced repeatedly in the debate about environmental needs.

Harden, like Ehrlich, took as his first premise that there was no technical solution to the "population problem" as it was then conceived. He thus rejected the panaceas of farming the seas or of the "green revolution" as in any way adequate to prevent the onrushing population catastrophy envisaged by Ehrlich and others.

He attributed the idea of the "tragedy" to its first publisher, William Foster Lloyd in 1833, thus acknowledging its age. The tragedy, in Harden's words, develops as follows:

> Picture a pasture open to all. It is to be expected that each herdsman will try to keep as many cattle as possible on the commons. Such an arrangement may work reasonably satisfactorily for centuries because tribal wars, poaching, and disease keep the numbers of both man and beast well below the carrying capacity of the land. Finally, however, comes the day of reckoning, that is, the day when the long-desired goal of social stability becomes a reality. At this point, the inherent logic of the commons remorselessly generates tragedy.
>
> As a rational being, each herdsman seeks to maximize his gain. Explicitly or implicitly, more or less consciously, he asks, "What is the utility to me of adding one more animal to my herd?" This utility has one negative and one positive component.
>
> 1) The positive component is a function of the increment of one animal. Since the herdsman receives all the proceeds from the sale of the additional animal, the positive utility is nearly +1.
>
> 2) The negative component is a function of the additional overgrazing created by one more animal. Since, however, the effects of overgrazing are shared by all herdsmen, the negative utility for any particular decision-making herdsman is only a fraction of -1.
>
> Adding together the component partial utilities, the rational herdsman concludes that the only sensible course for him to pursue is to add another animal to his herd. And another; and another. . . . But this is the conclusion reached by each and every rational herdsman sharing a commons. Therein is the tragedy. Each man is locked into a system that compels him to increase his herd without limit — in a world that is limited. Ruin is the destination

toward which all men rush, each pursuing his own best interest in a society that believes in the freedom of the commons. Freedom in a commons brings ruin to all.8

He describes pollution issues as a reverse example of the concept of the commons. Here, instead of taking something out of the commons, individuals put something in — pollution. The costs of purifying wastes are greater than the loss to the individual of contaminating the commons; thus, the rational person will continue to pollute. It is the same for each individual who makes that decision. The sum of the many individual rational decisions produces levels of pollution that are intolerable.

Harden's solutions to both (admittedly interlocked) problems of population and pollution are forms of "mutual coercion, mutually agreed upon."9 He acknowledges that the imposition of coercion (regulation) would be painful to some, but he justifies it on the grounds of general benefit.

TOWARD INTEGRATIVE CONCEPTS

As we have seen, for a long time, there have been people who regarded wilderness, and an unspoiled natural environment, as valuable in itself, without reference to the specific environmental issues that were of such high priority during the 1960s. These people respected the outdoors, and they were willing to go to great lengths to protect it as they knew it. They had formed a valuable support group for conservation in the past. Many such individuals together with others motivated by specific issues began in the 1960s to move toward the conceptualization of more general theories about people and the environment. Thus, emphasis was shifting somewhat from the specifics of poisonous pollution and population overcrowding to the effect of these factors on ecosystems and the interaction of social systems with these "natural" phenomena.

Barry Commoner wrote _The Closing Circle_,10 published in 1972, and _The Poverty of Power_,11 published in 1976, with these issues in mind. In the former, he dealt primarily with issues such as pollution that posed a threat to stable ecosystems. In the latter book, Commoner attempted to integrate the realms of ecology and political economy. A sample of text from _The Closing Circle_ helps to suggest his purpose:

The amount of stress which an ecosystem can absorb before it is driven to collapse is also a result of its various interconnections and their relative speeds of response. The more complex the ecosystem, the more suc-

> cessfully it can resist a stress. . . . Like a net, in which
> each knot is connected to others by several strands, such
> a fabric can resist collapse better than a simple un-
> branched circle of threads — which if cut anywhere
> breaks down as a whole. Environmental pollution is often
> a sign that ecological links have been cut and that the
> ecosystem has been artificially simplified.[12]

In _The Poverty of Power,_ his emphasis was on the economic system and the impact of the production of goods on the environment. He attempted to tie the social and economic systems, via waste, overconsumption, and so on, to the ecological crisis, concluding that there would be an eventual necessity for a planned, rational socialist government to deal with the issues. His efforts to develop an overriding analogy based on the second law of thermodynamics, including the uses of energy, efficiency, and work in the society seemed at best, to this writer, to be overstretching the parallels. Simplification has its values, but the limits of valid simplification for complex social interrelationships are quickly reached. Nevertheless, Commoner's books were widely read and quoted in the 1970s and can fairly be said to have influenced the direction of public thought.

Another example of the integrative approach came from Lynton Caldwell, a professor of political science in Indiana University. Beginning in about 1968, he expressed concerns about land use planning, stressing the need to base political decisions on an understanding of ecological systems. His journal article, "The Ecosystem as a Criterion for Public Land Policy," sought political decisions based on holistic views and scientific knowledge:

> The approach begins with an assumption based on
> scientific inquiry. The natural world is a composite of
> interrelating life-systems subsisting in a highly improbable
> terrestial environment. . . . [This brings about] the
> ultimate necessity of an ecosystems approach to environ-
> mental policy, including land, water, air and other
> substances upon which the human economy depends and the
> infinite character of human demands on the environ-
> ment . . . [what the law now needs to do is] to bring
> man-environment relationships into ecological balance.[13]

However much one may agree or disagree with the ideas of Ehrlich, Udall, Harden, and Commoner, or of the many others who contributed to the environmental debate, it is a fact that many of these people made significant contributions to the shaping of what we now call "the environmental ethic." In measured fashion, one after the other, they laid out the scientific knowledge that was available at the time, and they used it as a basis for conclusions about public policy.

While, in retrospect, it would have been foolish to deny the critical nature of our environmental problems, there are those who disagreed, and still disagree, with the "solutions" that emerged from the evidence of their writings. For, almost without exception, they adopted Garrett Harden's suggestion of "mutual coercion, mutually agreed upon." It was from this fabric that Congress was to fashion the adversarial control system that is the subject of this book.

The establishment of environmental controls was an act of political will, facilitated by the exercise of the pluralistic pressure that is so familiar in our unique democratic system. The unfolding of congressional interest and action, to be discussed in the next chapter, is a particularly instructive lesson in the use of that pluralism.

NOTES

1. Rachel Carson, _Silent Spring_ (New York: Houghton Mifflin, 1962), p. 5.

2. Stewart L. Udall, _The Quiet Crisis_ (New York: Holt, Rinehart and Winston, 1963), p. viii.

3. Paul R. Ehrlich, _The Population Bomb: Revised Edition_ (New York: Ballantine, 1968).

4. Ibid., p. 4.

5. J. H. Fremlin, "How Many People Can the World Support?," quoted in Ehrlich, _Population Bomb_.

6. Ehrlich, _Population Bomb_, p. 19.

7. Ibid., p. 26. The quotation from LaMonte Cole is from an address to the American Association for the Advancement of Science, December 27, 1967.

8. Garrett Harden, "The Tragedy of the Commons," _Science_ (December 13, 1968):1244.

9. Ibid., p. 1248.

10. Barry Commoner, _The Closing Circle_ (New York: Knopf, 1972).

11. Barry Commoner, _The Poverty of Power_ (New York: Knopf, 1976).

12. Commoner, _The Closing Circle_, p. 38.

13. Lynton Caldwell, "The Ecosystem as a Criterion for Public Land Policy," _Natural Resources Journal_ (October 1970):203.

3
Politics

It is important to any discussion encompassing both politics and the environment to distinguish between the various conceptual levels of environmental politics. While the political aspirations of environmentalists have been cast on a grand scale, right from the start, the effects of environmental pressures have often been rather limited and short term. Harvey Wheeler was pointing out in 1970 that there must be a macropolitical movement to effectuate "The Politics of Ecology."[1] The limited past efforts of conservationists were characterized as "the politics of tourism," and Wheeler advanced the view that future politics would be concerned first with the assessment of ecological balances and their effects on society, then only secondly with the social problems of poverty, crime, war, and the multitude of other imperatives that we are all so familiar with as the cruxes of contemporary political endeavor.

This view is in line with the political priorities of such organizations as the Green Party of West Germany and the Ecology Party of Great Britain. The human characteristics of such a social outlook were summed up by activist William L. Brian in 1975 in the following manner:

> An adequate and effective environmental movement must focus on resolving problems in the relationship between man and his natural environment in a way that will end human exploitation. Once the environmentalist has set overall humanitarian goals, he should follow the strategies of successful political activists, such as choosing a popular issue, building grassroots support, timing, crisis precipitation, flexibility, and openness to legal aid or negotiation. In short, the 'environmental' professional man

must become the 'political' man (or woman) in order to promote human welfare. . . .[2]

While such views were widely expressed in the 1960s and 1970s, the grand-scale ecological state of political consciousness that was so longed for by activists was not to be achieved during the period in which we are interested. What did come about, and with considerable force, was the consensus that "something is badly wrong with our environment and needs to be fixed." It is with the "fixing" then that this chapter is concerned.

As we have seen, the public became persuaded rather quickly in the 1960s that there was need for concern about the environment. Perceived social needs have traditionally been dealt with in the United States on two levels. First, there is public outcry about the issues and an opportunity for voluntary action by participants in the process. Second, after a period of consensus formation, there are demands for legislative action to redress the issues. This sequence has been evident in civil rights, unionization of labor, and many other fields. Because of the technical uniqueness and the genuine critical aspect of environmental issues, the time between initial demands and legislation to "fix" the environmental problems of the nation was shorter than in the examples mentioned above.

This speedy recompense was not achieved without the sincere and hard-working involvement of numerous individuals and pressure groups. The legislative counterparts of those agents of change were, of course, equally important in bringing about the national legal framework of environmental regulation that was to have both positive and negative effects on our society.

The purpose of this chapter, then, is to shed as much light as possible in this short space on those change aspects, and the process through which they worked, and hopefully to demonstrate the nature of the commitment to environmental values that persists today. In doing so, I will not be analyzing the issues as a political scientist, with the attendant theoretical constructs of that specialty, for I am not qualified to do so. Rather, I hope to describe the pressures of our pluralist society that have brought about the significant business and social changes inherent in environmental regulation, as well as the way in which compromises have been worked out on the way to national environmental policies.

Environmental groups, most with clever acronyms for names, were, of course, abundant in the early 1970s. Every college campus and almost every local community could boast its home-town organization to promote a better environment. The National Center for Voluntary Action estimated that in 1975 there were 40,000 environmental and conservation voluntary organizations in the United States. Most of these had little effect on the national political picture other than encouraging individual voters to make their voices heard. We are not concerned with these offshoots of the environmental enthusiasm of the nation in the aftermath of Earth Day and the other persuasions we are now familiar with. What seems important to me is that there were a substantial number of truly national and influential organizations attempting to sway national policy from about 1965 on.

Any list of these should include the following:

The Sierra Club
The National Audubon Society
The National Wildlife Federation
Environmental Action Inc.
The League of Conservation Voters
The Wilderness Society
The Environmental Defense Fund
The National Resources Defense Council
Friends of the Earth
The Isaak Walton League
Zero Population Growth

The two largest were the Sierra Club and the National Audubon Society. By 1974 the combined membership of these two organizations had risen to almost 400,000.

Most of these national groups were, by the mid-1970s, well financed and organized for their task along rather sophisticated lines. For example, the Sierra Club, with a national membership of 180,000 in 1977, maintained a full-time staff of 85 people. The Environmental Defense Fund, with a membership of 40,000 at about the same time, was administering a budget in 1976 of $1.3 million. In 1975 the Natural Resources Defense Council operated with a staff of 60 lawyers, scientists, and support personnel, with a budget of over $1.6 million.[3]

The Sierra Club is an interesting example of the national environmental organizations that have grown, stabilized, and continue to exert an influence on national environmental policy in the 1980s. The club, founded in 1892 by John Muir, was for many years as that signal association implies, a conservation organization. It is David Brower who probably deserves most credit for converting the organization from a regional conservation group into a national environmental lobby.

Between 1952 and 1969, Brower served as executive director and was responsible for an increase in membership from 7,000 to 85,000. Brower conceived most of the strategy that was to make the Sierra Club controversial, and in its way, successful. That strategy included the use of sensational full-page advertisements in major newspapers opposing legislation and federal projects and the litigation of issues that the club felt were within its purview as an environmental protector. It was one such program opposing a Bureau of Reclamation dam on the Colorado River that is said to have cost the club its nonprofit status. The Internal Revenue Service, in 1968, declared that the Sierra Club had become a lobby and thus had ceased to be a club entitled to tax-deductible contributions under IRS rules. The U.S. Supreme Court subsequently upheld the IRS in its ruling.

Brower and the club were active in campaigns to extend the size of redwood parks in California and of the Everglades in Florida. The club has edited and published 14 beautiful full-color books describing wilderness areas such as the Grand Canyon, Kauai, and Baja California. These books are expensive, and while they promote the image of the club, they raise money for the organization's coffers.

While the club operates without the benefit of tax deductibility of donations, several subsidiary organizations, separately incorporated, do qualify for that favorable status. For example, the Sierra Club Foundation now supports most of the club's educational, scientific, and literary activities. Another group, the Sierra Club Legal Defense Fund, underwrites nonlobbying legal activities.

The club has continued to grow since the departure of David Brower in 1969, and its current membership exceeds 180,000. Brower went on to found Friends of the Earth, an influential lobby for the environment.

The Sierra Club's activities continue to be varied and influential. It has played a key role in the ban on DDT, was active in the campaign to kill the SST supersonic aircraft, and lobbied to stop the poisoning of predators and to extend the nationally protected lands in California, Florida, and Alaska. It has been influential in the field of national energy policy and renewable sources of energy.

During the 1970s the club's legal defense fund played an important role in challenging the Trans-Alaska Pipeline, the California Water Project, the California Mineral King Ski area, the Palmdale, California, International Airport (near Los Angeles), and the Four Corners coal-burning power plants.

It is clear that the Sierra Club and other environmental organizations of its type played a pivotal role in the enactment of environmental legislation in the 1970s and that they continue to have the attention of many members of Congress.

There is little doubt that while the environmental groups were effective lobbies they would never have achieved their impact on public policy without the effect of "standing" in the federal courts. The idea that private groups should have the right to represent the public in litigation against the federal government and others was first advanced by consumer advocate Ralph Nader.

His public interest law group, the Center for the Study of Responsive Law, was founded in the mid-1970s and had an impact on consumer affairs through its ability to convince the federal courts that specific federal laws should be interpreted to allow a single group to represent the interests of the public, as plaintiffs. John F. Banzhaff III, followed Nader with a successful pro bon publico suit to force the Federal Communications Commission to ban cigarette commercials on radio and television, and in 1979 he founded an organization called Action on Smoking and Health (ASH) to further the cause of public health through litigation.

Roughly parallel to these actions, environmental groups were claiming, and winning, standing under different federal laws. They were to become, through the indulgence of the courts, almost private attorneys general seeking to protect the public interest in environmental matters. The landmark case in the issue of standing for environmental groups was the 1965 Scenic Hudson decision.[4] In that year, the Scenic Hudson Preservation Conference was granted standing to challenge the Federal Power Commission's licensing of a proposed power project at Storm King Mountain on the Hudson River. The Second Circuit Court held that a group with an interest in conservation should have the same rights as those representing economic matters and could be considered an "aggrieved" party. As such it was entitled to review under the provisions of the Federal Power Act. Environmental lawyers next convinced federal judges that the "fairness" provisions of the Administrative Procedures Act should allow the standing for "public interest" groups. They applied the logic of the Scenic Hudson decision in their successful claim that the noneconomic interest of environmental groups was in fact protected by the act, and thus they were entitled to standing as a possible aggrieved party.

This was followed in the years 1965-70 by successes with federal courts in the interpretation of federal highway and federal forestry statutes.[5] Thus, by 1970 the environmental lobby groups were in a position to challenge both specific applications of federal laws and regulations made under those laws, with respect to a number of federal statutes useful to their purposes. They were to use that influence as bargaining power in lobbying at the congressional level and to (often successfully) contest decisions of government agencies.

One rather disquieting aspect of all this is that the activity being described was being carried out in the name of the public by a rather select group of upper-middle-class lawyers and environmental organization officials. This has given rise on a number of occasions to the charge of "elitism" in the environmental movement. It was said that the activists involved drew both their financial and political support mainly from educated upper-class and upper-middle-class citizens and that blacks, poor people, and working men and women in general had little to gain from, or interest in, the environmental movement. In the words of one urban, poor black woman with four children, "What do I care for the forest, for the environment; I can't get out of the city and my children can't either."

A 1969 Gallup survey shed some light on the issue. According to the poll, the largest differences measured in attitudes toward environmental improvement were along the dimensions of education and income. College-educated people were more likely to favor an effort to clean up the environment than grade-school-educated respondents (62 percent versus 39 percent), and people with family incomes over $10,000 were likewise more concerned about the environment than those from families earning less than $5,000 (58 percent versus 41 percent).[6]

What this may say, however, is simply that people on the lower end of the socioeconomic scale had more urgent priorities than the environment at that time. The charge of "environmental elitism" is still heard, but it has not seriously damaged the progress of environmental reform and should not be considered here as a major political factor.

While the environmental groups were mounting an effective lobbying and litigative assault, starting about 1965, there were sympathetic forces at work in Congress that would ultimately bring about forms of regulation to meet their needs. Several important congressional leaders emerge as having played decisive roles in the shaping of environmental law. In the Senate, the principal actors were Senators Henry M. Jackson, Democrat of Washington, and Edmund S. Muskie, Democrat of Maine. The environmental forces in the House were led by Representative John D. Dingle, a Democrat from Michigan.

The strength of environmental sentiment in the Congress at the end of the 1960s can be illustrated by the size of the vote in the House in Favor of the National Environmental Policy Act (NEPA) when it reached the floor on September 23, 1969. The vote was 372 to 15 in favor of the act. This was the landmark piece of legislation for the entire period between 1965 and 1980, and the enactment of NEPA provides excellent insight into the strength and workings of the forces influencing environmental legislation at that time.

Though there has been a long incubation period for NEPA in the Senate Interior Committee, the act was to be catapulted into being by one of the ecological catastrophies that environmental groups had been predicting for years. The disaster was the Santa Barbara, California, oil spill, which occurred on January 28, 1969. The historical precedent to the Santa Barbara spill had been the traumatic grounding of the Union Oil tanker Torrey Canyon on a reef off of England's southern coast in March 1967. In the United States, viewers had watched spellbound as television crews photographed dying birds and sea life against a backdrop of oil-soaked beaches on the coasts of both England and France. When Torrey Canyon's counterpart occurred in California, the outcry was quickly translated into action in the Congress, and NEPA was the result.

The purpose of the act was to provide an overriding federal policy for the pursuit of environmental goals in the foreseeable future. It was followed later by more specific legislation to implement particular policies. The general tone of the endeavor was set by a statement by Senator Henry Jackson:

> A properly drafted Congressional statement of national environmental policy, along with a requirement for official statements of environmental findings in Federal decisions and legislative proposals, will effectively make the quality of the environment everyone's responsibility. . . . An environmental policy is a policy for people. Its primary concern is with man and his future. The basic principle of the policy is that we must strive, in all that we do, to achieve a standard of excellence in man's relationship to his physical surroundings.[7]

On the generalities of that statement, there was little to quarrel about within Congress or outside it chambers. With regard to the specifics of policy, considerable disagreement ensued. The first of these was a jurisdictional dispute between Senator Jackson and Senator Muskie. The Interior and Insular Affairs Committee, which Jackson chaired, had been considering how to articulate a national environment policy since late in 1967. During the summer of 1968, the committee published a report entitled <u>A National Policy for the Environment</u>,[8] which was prepared for the committee by Lynton K. Caldwell, a professor of government at Indiana University. The jurisdictional problems in the Senate developed between Jackson and Muskie over the authority of their respective committees, Jackson's Interior Committee and the Air and Water Pollution Subcommittee of the Senate Public Works Committee, of which Muskie was chairman. It must be remembered that both of these gentlemen had presidential ambitions in that year.

While Jackson was winning the jurisdictional battle in the Senate, the House was engaged in its own brand of NEPA discord. During this same period, the House Subcommittee on Science, Research, and Development had been studying the environmental problem with the consequent publication of the report, <u>Managing the Environment</u>. An environmental policy bill had also been introduced by Representative John Dingle through the sponsorship of the Fisheries and Wildlife Conservation Subcommittee of the Merchant Marine and Fisheries Committee. Clearance for debate on the floor of the House was dependent on a statement by the Rules Committee defining the boundaries of debate.

Objection to the debate ruling came from Wayne Aspinall, chairman of the House Interior Committee and an advocate of natural resource utilization on public lands. Aspinall felt that the bill's jurisdiction was in doubt and that the language proposed was too vague. He proposed amendments that its proponents felt would have gutted the bill. Though he was able to marshall considerable support for his views, his amendments were eliminated after lengthy maneuvering in conference and did not reach the floor of the House.

Perhaps the most critical period of the development of the law was provided by the testimony of Lynton Caldwell before Jackson's committee. Caldwell contended that for an environmental policy to be truly effective it must incorporate some "action-forcing mechanism." He insisted that there must be some means of evaluating environmental impacts and suggested the Bureau of the Budget as an enforcing agency to scrutinize impact statements for all federal projects. The idea, which was certainly discussed behind the scenes since Caldwell was a consultant to the committee, was accepted, and Senator Jackson sought to include provisions making all agencies responsible for the environmental impacts of their projects. Thus, the Federal Environmental Impact Statement, which would later be replicated in numerous state and local laws as the preferred modus operandi for environmental regulation, came into being.

NEPA has been called "the most important piece of environmental legislation that will ever be written." This assessment stems from its role as a guiding environmental policy, rather than, in most respects, a detailed enabling act. It was patterned after the Employment Act of 1946, with its provisions for a President's Council of Economic Advisors in the Office of the Executive and its many broad responsibilities for economic performance of the nation.

In its final form, NEPA contained three main provisions: a general statement of national environmental policy, requirements that federal agencies implement the policy, and the establishment of the Council on Environmental Quality in the Executive Office of the President. These are worth a more detailed look.

First, section 101 of Title I establishes a national policy for the environment.[9] It requires the federal government to use all reasonable means to employ the nation's resources judiciously. It specifically concerns itself with the environmental impact of "population growth, high-density urbanization, industrial exploitation, and . . . technological advances."

Second, section 102 of Title I requires all federal agencies to include the environmental consequence of decision making in their acts and to implement the national environmental policy "to the fullest extent possible." This section further requires that proposals for all major federal actions, including legislation, be accompanied by a detailed environmental statement, if those actions "significantly affect the quality of the human environment." Environmental statements are required to describe the following:

- The environmental impact of the proposed action.
- Any adverse environmental effects that cannot be avoided should the proposal be implemented.
- Alternatives to the proposed action.
- The relationship between local short-term uses of the environment and the maintenance and enhancement of long-term productivity.
- Any irreversible and irretrievable commitments of resources that would be involved in the proposed action should it be implemented.

Third, Title II of NEPA established the Council on Environmental Quality and sets forth its responsibilities. It calls for an annual environmental quality report to the president and the Congress, prepared by the council.

The passage of NEPA was followed in rapid sequence by the Clean Air Act of 1970 and the Federal Water Pollution Control Act (Clean Water Act) of 1972. In December 1970 Congress established the Environmental Protection Agency, which brought together many of the federal agencies responsible for pollution control. These included the Federal Water Quality Administration (from the Department of the Interior), the National Air Pollution Control Administration, the Bureau of Water Hygiene, and the Solid Waste Management Program (all from the Department of Health, Education and Welfare).

Thus, within the short period of three years, Congress brought into being the country's first comprehensive environmental policy, established the EPA as an overarching administrative body, and formulated specific policy in the areas of air and water pollution. The Clean Air Act and the Clean Water Act were to prove the most controversial of these actions. This was partly because they provided specific fixed emission standards, which were to prove so scientifically elusive, and because of their rigid administrative demands. Specific provisions of these laws will be considered later.

The outstanding political fact of this period is that the environmental lobbies, energized by the fervor of the nation for a better environment, were able to exert a decisive influence on Congress and that the public approved of that influence.

The passion for a clean environment was to undergo an important change as it was relegated to lower priority status with the arrival of the energy emergency precipitated by the OPEC oil embargo in 1973. It is tempting to speculate on the outcomes if legislative environmental efforts had been delayed a few years. Certainly the energy crisis of the mid-1970s would have played a strong role in shaping environmental law and would have complicated the political task of lobbyists and politicians alike. The energy crisis was, in fact, the decisive factor in persuading Congress to authorize the trans-Alaska pipeline in 1974 to bring North Slope oil to the seaport at Valdez, Alaska.

In this vein, most sociologists acknowledge that social movements in the United States tend to follow a life cycle pattern that includes emergence, growth, institutionalization, and eventually fragmentation and loss of influence.[10] There is substantial evidence, however, that this country's environmental movement is still a young movement — one that continues to exert considerable influence on the public. Though it must be admitted that the environment does not claim the high priority among voters that it once did, it nonetheless remains an important issue. One need only reflect on the resignation of Anne Burford as EPA administrator in March 1983 to find proof of the sensitivity that the Reagan administration feels to the political influence of environmental activists. The subsequent appointment, and unanimous Senate approval, of William Ruckleshaus to succeed Burford signaled a further desire on the part of the administration to avoid a congressional skirmish with environmentalists. Ruckleshaus, the founding administrator of the EPA, is widely regarded as reflecting the values of most environmental groups.

The administration's position was not taken without considerable evidence of the continued support of the public for the causes of environmental groups. For example, in 1980 the President's Council on Environmental Quality reported on a study commissioned by that council and several other federal agencies to ascertain the attitude of the public toward environmental matters. In the words of Gus Speth, the council chairman:

> Our purpose in commissioning the poll was to learn about key public opinion trends over the past decade, to obtain information about new areas of environmental concern and the degree of support for environmental protection, and to determine public responses to difficult choices between environmental protection and other values. . . .
>
> The survey found that the United States is, by and large, a nation which is willing to pay the price for environmental quality. We are a people deeply concerned about the presence of toxic chemicals in our environment. We want the government to test and regulate new chemicals before they are allowed on the market. . . . We still care very much about saving endangered species and pro-

tecting our fragile wetlands. On the other hand, while we still have a sustaining commitment to cleaning up air and water pollution and solving other environmental problems, they are no longer viewed as crisis issues by most Americans, whose top concerns now relate to inflation and the energy shortage."11

The study itself reports a significant proportion of the population favoring continued environmental vigilance, though not at the critical level of the early 1970s. When respondents were shown a list of ten major problems and asked the question ". . . which _three_ of these national problems would you like to see the government devote most of its attention to in the next year or two?" 24 percent included reducing pollution of air and water in the top three issues. This was in contrast to a 53 percent inclusion rate in a similar poll conducted in 1970 and 17 percent in 1965. In a more recent sampling of public opinion, Louis Harris and Associates conducted a study for _Business Week_ in January 1983. The public indicated a considerable growth in support for strong clean air and water laws since the last comparable Harris poll conducted in 1981. Questions about the Clean Air Act and the Clean Water Act, under review by Congress, indicated that support for even more stringent provisions of the acts had risen from 29 percent in 1981 to 47 percent in 1983 for clean air and from 53 percent in 1981 to 61 percent in 1983 for clean water.

What then is the status among citizens of the "crisis" issue of environmental protection? The available evidence shows quite clearly that two distinct facts affect the role of environmental issues, and their proponents, in determining national policy.

First, by 1980 the environment as an issue had receded from its role as the politically "hot" consideration that it was in the late 1960s and early 1970s. It had given way to the higher priorities of inflation, energy, and unemployment. All recent polls do, however, place the environmental issues among the top half-dozen national problems that voters want their government to respond to.

Second, the national environmental movement, embodied in environmental pressure groups and lobbies, has not diminished in strength. It continues to be a cohesive, well-financed set of organizations. These groups are respected by Congress and the media. They are capable of raising issues they feel need to be dealt with, and they see themselves as protectors of the environment, vigilant in the interest of their cause.

No stronger testimony to the ability to these groups and their congressional allies can be found than the demonstration of political pragmatism given by President Reagan when he decided to cut his losses at the EPA in March 1983 by replacing its director, the controversial Anne Burford, with William Ruckleshaus. It was clear to most political analysts that in anticipation of the 1984 presidential election the Republican Party deemed that it simply could not afford to engage in battle with the formidable combination of a hostile environmental movement and its supporters in Congress. The firing of Burford and six of the most senior officials who worked for her, together with the return of Ruckleshaus to government service to head the EPA, was a signal victory for environmentalists, who are, at the time of writing, cautiously optimistic about the future role of the EPA.

Thus, the environmental organizations, together with their legal auxiliaries, wait in the political wings, ready to prime the pump of public opinion in the interests of their causes. They are supported by a consensus that placed environmental issues high on the list, though not at the top, of public concern; and they are respected as a powerful political influence by both the Congress and the present national administration.

We can fully expect that these environmental organizations will continue to play an important role in the political affairs of the nation — to influence public policy and its application wherever the environment is concerned. Their mandate continues to be a consensus that the environment is important and that the federal government should be held responsible for protecting it. The "movement" has developed a modus operandi that works, and it cannot be expected to abandon it. For the foreseeable future, then, specific environmental organizations or clusters of them will have to be considered when national policy about the environment is suggested.

NOTES

1. Harvey Wheeler, "The Politics of Ecology," _Saturday Review_, March 7, 1970, p. 51.

2. William L. Bryan, "Toward a Viable Environmental Movement," _Journal of Applied Behavior Science_ 10 (March 1974):387.

3. Francis Sandbach, _Environment, Ideology and Policy_ (Montclair, N.J.: Allanheld, Osmund, 1980), p. 14.

4. Richard Liroff, _A National Policy for the Environment: NEPA and Its Aftermath_ (Bloomington: Indiana University Press, 1976), p. 151.

5. Ibid., p. 158.

6. J. McEvoy, "The American Concern With the Environment," in _Social Behavior, Natural Resources, and the Environment_, ed. W. R. Burch, N. H. Cheek, and L. Taylor (New York: Harper & Row), pp. 214-46.

7. Quoted in Odom Fanning, _Man and His Environment: Citizen Action_ (New York: Harper & Row, 1975), p. 38.

8. A special report to the Committee on Interior and Insular Affairs, U.S. Senate. Reprinted in U.S. Senate, National Environmental Policy, Hearing on S.1075, April 16, 1969, pp. 30-45.

9. 42 U.S.C. 4321 et seq., Pub. L. No. 91-190, 83 Stat. 852.

10. See, for example, A. L. Mauss, "On Being Strangled by the Stars and Stripes," Journal of Social Issues 27 (January 1971):183-202.

11. Council on Environmental Quality, Public Opinion on Environmental Issues (Washington, D.C.: Government Printing Office, 1980), p. 1.

PART II
U.S. ENVIRONMENTAL REGULATION TODAY

4
Environmental Costs and Benefits

Though U.S. citizens are nearly unanimous in their desire to enjoy a clean, healthful, and attractive environment, there have been numerous objections raised over the costs of delivering the kind of natural ambiance we would all like. Concerns have been most notably expressed by businesspeople and economists. The former are generally most anxious about the costs of operating their businesses under the rigid regulation required by the statutes regulating the environment, while the latter have protested about the implications of environmental regulation for increases in inflation rates and the reduction of productivity.

Considerable work has been done by economists, relating the costs of environmental regulation to the benefits, and it will be useful to look at some of the more significant studies and their conclusions.

At the outset, however, it is important to acknowledge that the use of technical and economic data in an effort to gain insight into the social prudence of a particular public policy decision by no means represents a foreclosure of the other dimensions along which such decisions are made. The importance of ethical and political factors in determining the course of government action has been discussed in the opening chapters of this book. These factors, plus the legal viewpoint, will always maintain a critical role in decisions made by public officials in their efforts to balance environmental needs. It is equally true that the quantitative analysis of costs and benefits generally provides additional insights into the efficacy of policy.

Lester Lave has described the fallacy of ignoring quantitative effects in the formulation of social policy in his evaluation of the Clean Air Act of 1970. He points out:

For example, Congress set specific emission standards for automobiles in the Clean Air Act Amendments of 1970. With virtually no data on control costs, air quality, or health effects, Congress mandated a 90 percent reduction in emissions of each pollutant. The legislation fails to recognize that some pollutants are more harmful or more costly to abate than others and that abating emissions carries with it costs in accomplishing other social goals, such as better fuel economy. The amendments were strongly influenced by ethical, legal and political views, but their authors rejected technical-economic frameworks. As might be expected, the legislation had solid ethical and political appeal but proved impossible to implement as written; what was implemented was costly, a continuing source of controversy, and subject to numerous delays. One danger of regulations based on ethics and political power is that they may be obsolete before they are implemented due to shifts in public consensus. Thus economic difficulties in the automobile industry in 1980 caused many regulations to be suspended. There is nothing wrong with revising regulatory decisions in the face of new evidence; automobile emission regulations, however, have been revised almost annually in a government-business confrontation that damages institutions and delays achieving clean air.[1]

The history of cost-benefit analysis can be traced to the 1930s when the federal government began to measure the potential effects of some programs in quantitative terms. The Army Corps of Engineers was among the first to employ these methods in evaluating their projects. Much of the early work was haphazard, however, and data collection lacked the rigor that is demanded today. The fledgling discipline was subject to constant pressure to justify political decisions, and the respectability of cost-benefit analysis has been cast in doubt at various times as a result. Nonetheless, continued improvements and the adaptation of the methodology by industry for a broad range of projects has given cost-benefit studies the respectability they deserve, and currently the basic methodology is widely used.

In 1974 the EPA published its own cost studies in an attempt to quantify clean air and water costs for the Congress. That report, <u>The Cost of Clean Air and Water,</u> was to be accompanied by a large nongovernment body of literature on the subject. Thus, we are now in a position to know quite a lot about the costs and benefits of government regulation to protect the environment.

Before considering the data from some of those studies, however, we should look at some definitions, as well as some of the limitations of quantitative analysis in the environmental field. Fundamental to all analyses of this sort is the concept of "externalities." A good description of externalities is provided by Kneese and Herfindahl:

> . . . what a consumer consumes or what a business firm uses is not entirely within its control. That is, there are flows of some goods or services that come to the consumer or business whether he wants them or not and without his paying for them. This situation may be described by saying that a change in the output of one economic unit (a firm or consumer) necessarily affects the inputs (and hence the output) of some other economic unit. That is, the activities of one economic unit may generate "real" effects that are external to it. These effects are often called external effects, or "externalities." For example, an increase in the output of a cannery may increase stream pollution, which in turn will require downstream firms or communities to spend more money to clean up the water they use. They have experienced an unwanted increase of certain inputs — pollutants in this case. . . . If external effects are present, a misallocation of resources is likely to be the result whether the external effect is beneficial or detrimental to its recipient. The reason for this is that the signals which tell a firm how much it should produce — price and cost — may not work properly in the presence of external effects . . . these may be generated and received by any pair of economic units. Smith's record player may disturb Jones' rest. Or their cars may slow each other and other drivers on the way to work. We may swim in or picnic alongside water that has been polluted by businesses, individuals, or even governmental units.[2]

The regulation of environmental pollution by government, then, can be seen as the process of eliminating or controlling externalities.

While that concept is simple, the decision to control or eliminate specific externalities will rest on the relative values of the costs produced by the externalities and the benefits of eliminating them. It is in the measurement of these costs and benefits that we encounter trouble. The difficulties on the cost side fall into four categories: difficulty in measuring and predicting costs with any degree of precision; the worrisome tendency of abatement costs to escalate dramatically when attempting to eliminate the last few parts per million of any contaminant in air or water (this is sometimes called the hockey-stick syndrome); the impact of timing; and our assiduous practice of making assumptions about technology.

The first of these, problems with cost measurement, will have a familiar ring to most businesspeople. While it may be a simple task to "cost out" the installation of a particular piece of pollution control equipment, the effectiveness of a device will not usually be known in advance with certainty when it comes to any specific installation, since the inputs to that equipment will tend to vary with each industrial process. Further, the instant imposition of regulations on an entire industry, or several industries, will often produce a shortage of certain types of equipment with the usual changes in price and delivery conditions. For example, if a regulation calls for control that because of current technology is heavily dependent on a particular process, components that the process uses, say pumps, will experience a sudden demand. The resultant overtime required in the pump industry and the possibility of added base-wage demands by workers will often drive up the price of pumps, as well as interfering with deliveries. The ripple effect produced in this way is very difficult to estimate in advance.

From the point of view of the regulatory agency, any attempt to estimate the costs to industry of imposing a specific regulation must also take this ripple effect into account. It is not enough to simply calculate the cost of a piece of abatement equipment and multiply that cost by the number of producers in the regulated industry. The problem takes on larger proportions when one considers the long-term cumulative impacts of a series of interrelated regulations.

The costs of eliminating pollution have been empirically shown to exhibit an interesting and perplexing characteristic, which is sometimes dubbed "the hockey-stick syndrome." Picture a hockey stick placed so that the contact blade is pointing upward on the right, and the long handle is sloping up from left to right in a gentle rise from the horizontal. Now, if increasing percentages of air and water purity are described on a horizontal axis just below the stick handle with 100 percent purity just to the right of the vertical blade of the stick, and if the cost of achieving varying percentages of cleanliness are described ascending on a vertical axis placed just to the right of the blade, we have a graph with a hockey-stick-shaped curve relating costs to purity.

The graph will show that as we increase cleanliness of air or water for almost any contaminant, from zero to say 85 percent, the cost will rise gradually (as the handle of the stick slopes upward). Then when we attempt to increase purity by a few extra percentage points, the cost will move up the blade area of the "stick curve" and will escalate rapidly. As we approach the last few points of cleanliness, generally above 99 percent clean, the shape of the curve is exponential, rising almost vertically. In fact, for most contaminants, the very last part per million of pollution can be removed only at an unknown cost, suggesting that the cost may in fact be infinite for totally clean air or water on a large scale.

These relationships have been shown to hold for a very wide range of contaminants. As an example of the problems created by the estimation of costs in the exponential range of the curve, consider the results of an early EPA study of the costs of water treatment.[3] The study estimated that eliminating 85 to 90 percent of all contaminants in water in the United States would cost $61 billion in the decade from 1971 to 1981. Increasing purity to a range of 95 to 99 percent for all effluent would increase costs to $119 billion. If we were to remove 100 percent of impurities from only one-fifth of the waste water while keeping the remainder 95 to 99 percent clean, costs were estimated at $157 billion. If we then went the additional step to 100 percent removal of contaminants from all wastes, the cost was estimated at $317 billion.

The study did not consider the effects of urban runoff, agricultural wastes, or mine wastes. Further, the study made technological assumptions that have since been cast in doubt, particularly with respect to the highest levels of discharge waste removal. It is generally conceded, at the time of writing, that it is impossible to reach a zero discharge (no pollution) level. Nevertheless, the study, as has others, serves to point out the precarious relationship that costs bear to benefits in the higher ranges (probably above 98 percent) of pollution control.

The relationship of costs to deadlines imposes another uncertainty on most cost-benefit calculations. Much as I have described in the ripple effect caused by regulations, short deadlines, often written into law, can be responsible for cost increases or uncertainty. A good example of this can be seen in the automobile industry, where deadlines imposed by the Clean Air Act of 1970 virtually precluded the long-term option of developing a vehicle power plant that would serve as an alternative to the internal combustion engine. In order to attempt meeting the deadlines, the industry was required to embark on a series of "quick fixes" consisting of attachments to existing engines. These were not only costly, a fact brought home to the consumer at the showroom floor, but in many cases their imposition interfered with other policy priorities of the federal government. Fuel economy, for example, has been seriously handicapped by the long string of gadgets attached to U.S. engine blocks for the purpose of meeting requirements of the Clean Air Act.

Of primary concern here is the manner in which costs can be virtually dictated by the actions mandated in legislation. While the best method or technology may suggest one set of costs, either for the short term or for more long-range purposes, it is often political considerations that determine what the public will ultimately pay for its clean environment. The automobile case cited above is but one of many in this category.

Underlying almost all environmental control legislation, and some regulations, are assumptions about the technology that will be forthcoming to facilitate compliance with the law. The technology of 1985 will not serve the needs of the environment in the year 2000. We must continuously make assumptions about the development of technology to meet needs without knowing that proper technical resources will be available to do the job. If we attempt to estimate the costs of providing, say, automobile exhausts free of oxides of nitrogen, we must start the calculation with a statement of the abatement method to be employed. When the solution to the problem exists only in the hypothesis stage, this cannot be done. We may provide a range of possible costs, or even a probabilistic statement based on promising technologies, but experience with developing technologies has shown that this is a long way from the clear-cut statement of the costs of eliminating externalities that is so often visualized in the legislative process.

Both the Clean Air Act and the Clean Water Act attempted to bypass this problem by requiring the EPA to set emission standards for stationary pollution sources based on "adequately demonstrated" technology or "best available" technology. The record demonstrated that EPA, with limited budgets and little access to the expertise in industry, was not much better at envisioning technological costs than Congress was.

While attempts to arrive at meaningful estimates on the cost side of the cost-benefit equation present serious problems, there is certainly a much more widespread perception of the enormous difficulties inherent in estimating the value to society of the social _benefits_ arising from the elimination of externalities. As an example, consider the plight of the economist who, called on to clarify a cost-benefit relationship at an offshore oil conference in 1975, attempted to monetize the existence of one seagull. One gull's life was worth "no more than ten dollars," he estimated. Environmentalists were livid. Jacques Cousteau attacked the man with venom, for failure to understand the "value of life itself"[4] (so much for estimating the value of life).

Most would agree that we should not spend vast sums from either the public or private purse cleaning up air or water beyond the degree that it is harmful; however, the degree of harm and the level that we can tolerate must be subject to the closest scrutiny. This has been the job of the EPA in most environmental cases, and it has changed its mind several times on this score — as well it should, in light of new evidence. The literature on air pollution effects, for example, is a maze of laboratory studies, epidemiological studies, and longitudinal studies of groups, many of them presenting conflicting conclusions regarding the pollution levels at which one can expect the onset of episodes in asthma sufferers and other sensitive individuals.[5] While the EPA must decide the level of pollutants that the regulations will tolerate, related to the health effects, the reduction of those pollutants is clearly not a benefit that we need, or want, to monetize. The fact that the benefit is a desirable goal for society must then be determined on largely ethical and partly political grounds. If it is clear that we cannot agree on the monetary value of the life of a seagull, then we certainly must remove the far more weighty considerations involving human life and health to another venue.

Damage to wildlife and ecological systems is another incalculable cost of environmental pollution. Its abatement is likewise a benefit difficult to monetize.

In fact, many observers have recently taken the position that to attempt to calculate the monetary value of most social benefits may be at worst ludicrous and at best unnecessary. Allen Ferguson, who is of this school, declares:

> By and large it is not necessary, in my judgment, to monetize benefits. It is frequently very useful, but it is more frequently unnecessary. What do you need to do if you do not need to monetize benefits? What we need to do is get some ideas of benefits by first determining what the effect of the regulation would be. Some regulation is flat out counterproductive — it does not accomplish what it is intended to do; it may even, in some cases, make the situation worse. In any event, one has to ascertain the direct impact of the regulation. Does the regulation reduce sulfur dioxide in the air? Does it reduce the exclusion of people from the marketplace? Does it reduce fuel consumption? What is its direct effect? That is a link that often gets overlooked in discussion of the value of regulation. One assumes that the regulation does what it is supposed to do. Then one has to look at how the society responds to that effect. Is there a reduction in the carcinogen in food? What population is affected? What is the vulnerability of the population? How big is that group? What are their characteristics? And, then, what is it about that group that is affected? Do you decrease their expected morbidity? Do you increase their life expectancy? Do you decrease their sense of alienation? Do you reduce their political dependence — the political dependence of the United States — on Arab oil? What is the consequence of the regulation?
>
> Now, that is where the analysis can end in most cases. The decision maker in deciding whether to insist on a particular action should ideally make some kind of a judg-

ment, for example, that the best available evidence indicates that this regulation will reduce loss of lives due to some particular ailment by perhaps 100–5000 per year. That is about the best range of accuracy you can reasonably expect, one or two orders of magnitude. In the case of saccharin, the estimates of vulnerability to cancer through consuming saccharin range over seven orders of magnitude. We have done all the work, and we say now here is this activity that may save 100–5000 lives per year. We do not need to say . . . and those lives are worth 8000 or 80,000 or 800,000 dollars each. All we need to do is say, is it worth N millions of dollars or N billions of dollars to increase the prospect of reducing loss of life by that magnitude.[6]

As Ferguson has suggested, there are, of course, some areas of benefit that yield rather well to the calculation of monetary terms. While these are seen by most economists as relatively less important than the critical health and ecological effects, they are nevertheless worth considering in most contexts. They include, largely, the avoidance of costs caused by pollution in addition to costs that are no longer there when pollution is abated, such as corrosion and surface damage to paint and other architectural materials, as well as damage to crops and plantings. These may be conveniently calculated by measuring the cost of replacing the things that pollution would have destroyed, had it been there. Considerable stress has been placed on these factors by European governments in their consideration of pollution controls. An Organization for Economic Cooperation and Development (OECD) estimate of many of these costs was published in 1974 and has been widely cited.[7] In the United States, however, the health and ecological effects have so outweighed the benefits that can be monetized as to dwarf them in policy considerations. On the whole, while I feel that rigor calls for the calculation of all costs and benefits that can reasonably be monetized in any regulatory decision, I concur with Ferguson.

This is not to say that _costs_ of social programs, in particular environmental programs, should not be calculated. The budgetary need to compare one program in terms of cost with another at the legislative level is certainly reason enough to surmount the difficulties that have been pointed out in the quantification of costs. One should keep in mind, though, that when attempting that kind of computation the numbers must be subject to the most severe skepticism. Further, the public is entitled to an understanding of the external economic effects inherent in expenditures for environmental purposes. Very large expenditures on environmental programs affect investment in projects that would otherwise improve productivity, and they certainly have significant impact on the interrelationship of one industry to another, including employment factors. We need to know, then, what environmental regulation is costing us, both in relation to our other priorities, such as defense and welfare, and in its impact on our economy; for, after all, economic factors, as well as environmental factors, have a great deal to do with the quality of our life.

The actual costs of environmental protection in the United States have been recorded rather carefully by the U.S. Department of Commerce, Bureau of Economic Analysis, since 1972. These outlays, which include business annual costs and investment, and expenditures by governmental units in current dollars from 1972 to 1981 are indicated below.[8]

```
1972 . . . $18.43 billion
1973 . . .  21.93 billion
1974 . . .  26.26 billion
1975 . . .  30.92 billion
1976 . . .  34.68 billion
1977 . . .  37.96 billion
1978 . . .  43.01 billion
1979 . . .  49.19 billion
1980 . . .  55.66 billion
1981 . . .  61.33 billion
```

It is clear that in the years 1972 through 1976 environmental regulation was a growth industry, but annual increases in expenditures have not been uniform by any means. The longer-term trend indicates a declining rate of growth with stabilization over the most recent years. The percentage change over the previous year in real pollution and abatement expenditures (adjusted for inflation) has been:

```
1973 . . . 12 percent
1974 . . .  3 percent
1975 . . .  8 percent
1976 . . .  6 percent
1977 . . .  2 percent
1978 . . .  5 percent
1979 . . .  1 percent
1980 . . .  0 percent
1981 . . . -1 percent
```

Clearly, early growth rates were the result of new regulations, while more recent annual increases in expenditures, though dampened by the 1979-82 recession, probably reflect a leveling off of these outlays as more basic sources of environmental degradation come close to satisfactory levels of discharge.

Continued regulatory activity with its associated costs to industry and the consumer must be expected; perhaps there will be significant new initiatives in the area of solid waste or atomic waste disposal. It seems safe, however, to speculate that present levels of annual expenditure, in the neighborhood of $60 billion (at 1981 levels) annually, will be sufficient to provide a realistic environmental system for the country in the near future.

At these levels, we are spending more than most other industrial countries to protect our environment. In terms of both percentage of business expenditures and in relation to gross national product, we spend more than any other country except Japan. While public sector expenditures for pollution abatement are not readily available for most industrial countries, the private sector investment is recorded by the Organization for Economic Cooperation and Development. The OECD figures for 1975, for example, are shown in Table 4.1.[9]

TABLE 4.1
Private Sector Expenditure
for Pollution Abatement (1975)

	Investment, Percent of GDP*	Percent of Total Private Investment
United States	0.44	3.4
Japan	1.00	4.6
Denmark	0.17	0.9
Finland	0.22	0.9
France	0.28	1.4
West Germany	0.32	1.9
Netherlands (1974)	0.22	0.9
Norway	0.22	0.7
Sweden	0.19	1.1
United Kingdom	0.29	1.7

*gross domestic product

The impact of expenditures at this level on the United States' economic welfare has been the subject of widespread debate. There are differential impacts of regulation, with the burden of cleanup dealing an almost crushing blow to some sectors of the economy, while lightly brushing others. Thus, the metals and chemical industries have suffered acute economic hardship in an effort to provide what can be seen objectively as fairly moderate results. There is still a long way to go in these areas, and the costs of curbing pollution to satisfactory levels will take continued enormous expenditures in the future. One can hardly blame managers in those industries for harboring some bitterness over the sledgehammer impact of regulations. On the other hand, the effect of environmental regulation on the economy as a whole is beginning to be understood as a fairly moderate influence. In recent years fairly sophisticated data have been collected, and economic simulations that supply a reasonable measure of confidence in the future have been developed. Thus, results of studies such as that produced in 1978 by the EPA and the President's Council on Environmental Quality, "The Macroeconomic Impact of Federal Pollution Control Programs," covering the period from 1970 to 1986 in simulation, have gained acceptance as representing a reasonable view of economic impacts. The latter study imputes an average 0.4 percent rise in wholesale prices per year to environmental controls. It also forecasts a reduction in gross national product averaging 0.3 percent per year over the period, as a result of those controls.

No one can deny that even these fractional percentages represent a significant effect or that the $380 billion spent from 1972 to 1982 is a staggering sum. One must not forget, however, that we are talking here about costs versus benefits. Thus, the most important aspect of any analysis must be whether the cost has purchased acceptable benefits for the outlay.

From the social and political standpoint, the best measure of whether we are purchasing desirable results with our environmental expenditures is the public consensus. On that score, the polls show a very clear preference. The public does not want a reduction in environmental protection, even if the savings would secure some economic improvement. Representative of samplings is a Roper poll conducted in September 1979.[10] Sixty-five percent of respondents said either they felt the balance between costs and benefits was about right or that we do not yet have enough environmental protection, while 24 percent felt that laws and regulations had become too expensive. More recently, a Harris poll conducted for **Business Week** in January 1983 measured the public approval of stricter clean air and clean water legislation.[11] Harris found that support for cleaner air has risen since 1981 from 29 to 47 percent and that for cleaner water public approval has risen from 52 percent in 1981 to 61 percent in the 1983 poll. Americans are thus aware that there is a significant cost associated with pollution control and other environmental regulation, but they seem satisfied that the cost is reasonable in relationship to the benefits.

What conclusions, then, can be drawn about the relationships of costs to benefits in the environmental regulation field? The following are mine.

First, while we can adequately, but with some difficulty, monetize the costs brought about by environmental regulation, to do so for the social benefits that result is, except in a handful of cases, both unnecessary and foolish. We should no more try to express the benefits of a clean environment in dollars than we should attempt to calculate the benefit to the nation of a hot school lunch for a child. The major benefits, while very real, cannot be expressed in monetary terms. We must then compare the costs of a clean environment with a package of benefits that, while nonmonetary, have a very real value.

Second, we have made good progress in recent years in calculating those costs, both in absolute terms, and in their effect on the economy. The effects on specific industries are more worrisome to me than the impact on the economy as a whole. The costs in terms of increased inflation and reduced productivity thus seem reasonable in return for the overall benefits attributed to a cleaner environment.

Those overall benefits must, in real-world terms, be measured by the satisfaction of the electorate with the cost-benefit balance. This is a political matter then, not solely an economic consideration, though economics must, in my view, play an important role in quantifying the issues as best possible.

Finally, the electorate seems to have expressed its satisfaction, in general terms, with the balance of costs and benefits we have achieved. This is attested to by both the polls cited above and by the fact that voters continue to reelect members of Congress, in substantial numbers, who strongly advocate environmental regulation continuing at least at the present level. It is probably because of this continued support for environmental regulation by the electorate that most business leaders now agree with the general consensus on environmental goals. How we should achieve those goals and what we should do about the exaggerated effects of regulation on several specific industries is not nearly so clearly agreed upon.

NOTES

1. Lester B. Lave, <u>The Strategy of Social Regulation</u> (Washington, D.C.: Brookings Institution, 1981), p. 131.

2. A. V. Kneese and O. C. Herfindahl, "Tools and Analyzing Environmental Problems," in <u>Economic Thinking and Pollution Problems,</u> ed. D. A. L. Auld (Toronto: University of Toronto Press, 1972), p. 14.

3. A. V. Kneese and C. L. Schultz, <u>Pollution, Prices, and Public Policy</u> (Washington, D.C.: Brookings Institution, 1975), p. 78.

4. G. C. Hill, "Off-shore Oil Stirs Heated Debate," _Wall Street Journal_, September 9, 1975, p. 1.

5. For a more detailed discussion of this subject, see Lave, _Social Regulation_, pp. 103-20 and references cited.

6. James F. Gatti, _The Limits of Government Regulation_ (New York: Academic Press, 1981), p. 153.

7. Organization for Economic Cooperation and Development, _Environmental Damage Costs_ (Paris: OECD, 1974).

8. Gar L. Rutledge and Susan Lease-Trevanthan, "Pollution Control and Abatement Expenditures, 1972-81," _Survey of Current Business_ 63 (February 1983).

9. Organization for Economic Cooperation and Development, _The State of the Environment in OECD Member Countries_ (Paris: OECD, 1979), p. 134.

10. For information about a number of polls conducted on this issue, see Council on Environmental Quality, _Public Opinion on Environmental Issues_ (Washington, D.C.: Government Printing Office, 1980).

11. "A Call for Tougher — Not Weaker — Antipollution Laws," _Business Week_, January 24, 1983.

5
Business and Government in Conflict: The Adversarial Relationship

During the waning months of the Carter administration, I lunched with a few colleagues and the chief executive of one of this country's largest corporations. This man told a tale of intrigue involving the EPA and his company that is worthy of at least a grade-B spy thriller.

The firm developed a proprietary chemical process that enabled it to cut the production cost of certain elements of one of its major products. The firm was understandably zealous in its protection of what it regarded as a valuable trade secret. Somehow, the local office of the EPA found out about the process and requested that EPA be allowed to examine the new equipment to determine if it produced excessive air pollution. While our luncheon companion insisted that the process operated within established regulations, the company refused to allow EPA personnel to inspect the equipment on the grounds that such information was proprietary, and it did not wish it to be placed in the EPA files where it would be available to its competitors under the Freedom of Information Act. The company suggested that emissions be checked at the company fence line, which was customary in any case, and had been the practice with other equipment the firm operated. The managers did not see why this particular process should be made an exception.

Officials at the EPA demurred. They then filed suit in federal court, asking that they be allowed to inspect the process. The court upheld the company and instructed the EPA to follow its usual "fence line" practice of determining if the company was producing excessive pollution. At this point, our informant thought the incident had ended.

A short time later, one of the company's engineers noticed a light aircraft circling at low altitude over the plant where the new process operated. Part of this was outdoors. Being suspicious, he was able to note the identification numbers on the plane's wing. Thinking this might be a competitor, the engineer had the aircraft traced to a local charter flying service.

When the operators were asked who had chartered the plane, the response was surprising — an employee of the EPA! The company's lawyers, knowing just where to look, evoked the Freedom of Information Act to examine the EPA files pertaining to this particular plant. And, sure enough, there they were — 8"X10" glossies of the firm's "secret" process equipment right where the whole world could find them.

That these photos, in the hands of a government agency, might cost the firm its competitive advantage seemed to all of us, including the company's chief executive, somewhat less important than the obvious principles involved.

I tell this story, not to prove that there are scoundrels in the EPA (there probably are, just as there are scoundrels in business and every other walk of life) but to illustrate something of the climate of distrust and hostility that exists between industry and government agencies charged with protecting the environment. I would like to be able to say that this has all changed with the Reagan administration, but lamentably this is not the case. That issue will be examined at some length in a later chapter. The point of this story is that our chief executive certainly is not going to trust EPA very much in the future. In fact, this particular firm now often proceeds directly to the courts in its dealings with regulatory agencies. As we will see, that course of action has its drawbacks as well.

It must be clear that any time government attempts to regulate our lives there will be some resentment on the part of those who are regulated. The need of individuals to be free of government constraints is one of the powerful intuitive appeals of Libertarianism and has spawned political movements down through the ages. While the world body politic includes literally dozens of movements that appeal to this need, U.S. citizens are thought to be among the most individualistic of people. We thus frequently express, through our personal and political choices, a value for limiting government intervention in our lives.

It is the thesis of a number of popular writers, most notably television commentators, that the hostility existing between business and government today is simply an extension, albeit an exaggerated one, of this "don't mess with me" strain in the American character.[1] This point of view holds that U.S. business regards profits, undeniably a dominant value in corporate life, as the inalienable right of business and considers government regulation to be an intrusion into some red-necked domain of enterprise privilege. That this premise is so seldom challenged speaks both of the lack of organization of the business community in its own interest and of the low esteem in which business is currently held by the public.

While I do not propose to deny that there are some individuals in industry who fit this simplistic media stereotype, common sense as well as scores of discussions with executives over the years have absolutely convinced me that the phenomenon of adversarial conflict between business and government is a much more complex issue and deserves careful definition. We just cannot deal with the destructive effects of this ongoing antagonism without some clear understanding of its origins and of the motor that drives it.

How has it been possible for intelligent, dedicated public servants and some of the country's best trained, most thoughtful business leaders to come to the conclusion that the first assumption in mutual dealings is that of villainy, each for the other?

The answer has historical, legal, and value-based roots. We did not arrive where we are without precedent, and today's positions are not maintained without prejudice.

Industry has been regulated in the United States for quite a long time. While there have been regulations of a minor sort for as long as there have been government entities in this country, most historians mark the emergence of federal controls over business with the start of the Progressive Era, roughly coincidental with Theodore Roosevelt's election as president in 1901. The primary concern at that time was business interrelationships that burdened the economy with manipulation seen as detrimental to consumers and small business.[2] The antitrust legislation of the period, together with the vigorous Progressive posture of Theodore Roosevelt in pursuing redress of detrimental business arrangements, gave many business leaders cause for concern about future business-government relations. During that period, journalists turned to muckraking, which some now say is an honored tradition, to engage the attention of the public and stimulate an appetite for reforms. While the targets of the muckrakers were relatively few individuals, there were many who from a loyalty to economic class, or out of economic necessity, felt concern about the direction that government was taking. The time span of the Progressive movement was limited. As a political force, it was virtually exhausted by 1914. I would suggest that no detailed analysis of Progressivism and its effect on government-business relations would be complete without inclusion of the well-documented role of the muckrakers.[3] The tensions between government and business, which were to later be thought of as traditional, had their start in this period.

Though the Progressive movement had lost much of its attraction to U.S. politics by 1914, the appointment by Woodrow Wilson of Louis D. Brandeis to the Supreme Court in 1916 was seen as a Progressive gesture, and the passage by Congress of workman's compensation and child labor legislation in the same year represented a continuation of the trend. The foreign policy issues that preoccupied the later stages of the Wilson administration moved public interest away from the regulation of business, and this emphasis was not to return until the era of President Franklin D. Roosevelt and the New Deal.

With the impetus of the economic depression of the 1930s, the administration of Franklin D. Roosevelt turned to business reform and further economic regulation. The face of the New Deal with its Fair Labor Standards Act, National Recovery Act, National Labor Relations Act (the Wagner Act), and the establishment of the controversial National Labor Relations Board under that act, was unacceptable to many businesspeople, who saw government intruding still further into private decision processes. It was during the New Deal that businesspeople in substantial numbers, representing both large and small enterprises, began to think of the federal government as an adversary.

Regulations of the New Deal and Progressive Eras were characterized by several common elements. In general, these were not to be duplicated in any future regulation. First, they dealt primarily with economic issues. Antitrust, labor, and transportation regulation are examples of the economic thrust of public concern about the role of business.[4] Second, many were one-industry regulations, and the administrators in the federal government were specialists in the industry for which they had oversight. Thus, the Interstate Commerce Commission regulated railroads, the Civil Aviation Board, airlines, and the Federal Drug Administration, the drug business.

The wave of business regulation, which emerged in the 1960s and reached such enormous proportions in the 1970s, did not generally share these common factors. It was quite different in a number of ways. First, it can fairly be said to be _social_ regulation of business[5] as opposed to the economic brand of legislation of the previous eras. That is, it strove to modify the social behavior of business rather than the economic, as had previously been the case. Social behavior included the actions of business toward consumers and toward the environment, but actions that affected rather vaguely defined conditions. Thus, Congress strove to define what was "fair" lending on the part of banks and attempted to classify "safe" usages of products. Again "clean" air and water have been the subject of contentious discussion for many years now. The question is quite fairly asked, "how clean is clean enough?" Further, rather than regulation on a single-industry basis, most of the newer laws control activities of a large number of industries, cutting across markets and industrial processes. The EPA, for example, is responsible for establishing and enforcing regulations for an enormously disparate range of businesses from steel making to local cleaning shops.

In addition to the fact that regulators must now deal with a wide range of industry, with little opportunity to become expert in any one, George Steiner has pointed out that the newer social regulations of industry are operated from a "command-and-control" posture that allows for little or no flexibility in the application of rules.[6] The new regulators, rather than ruling on the suitability of proposals made by industry, come complete with ready-made regulations that must be obeyed and within time limits specified by Congress or the regulations themselves.[7] I have said quite a lot about this feature of environmental regulation. I have suggested, and repeat here, that it is one of the major contributors to the adversarial relationship between business and government.

It is worth noting that this command posture is not an element of regulation generally shared by other industrial countries. European enforcement is a mosaic of consultative techniques ranging from cooperative standard setting to economic incentives for performance. More will be said of this later; in particular, the British consultative experience will be examined in detail in Chapter 7. The Japanese experience is also quite different. The implementation of pollution regulations — which do rely on national emission standards — is largely the responsibility of local officials. These regulators work within a philosophy described as "administrative guidance," which actually involves considerable flexibility with a number of standards being negotiated, set, and implemented on a case-by-case basis at the local level.[8]

The importance of these local officials can be seen from the fact that of the total number of individuals employed in pollution control in Japan in 1974, 93 percent were retained at the prefecture (regional) and municipal levels. The remaining 7 percent, or less than 1,000 employees, directed national government efforts.[9]

The most important thing to keep in mind about Japanese environmental regulation is that the spirit as well as the practice of "administrative guidance" is persuasion rather than coercion. In spite of the fact that applicable laws do carry severe penalties for violations, Japanese courts record virtually no cases of enforcement by the judiciary.

How then did U.S. environmental regulation, with its heavy-handed overtones for adversarial relationships, come to depart so radically from the relatively smooth course chosen by our national industrial counterparts? One element of the answer can be seen in the decline of U.S. public approval of business. This phenomenon, incidentally, applies as well to other social regulation of the 1960s and 1970s.

The earliest known poll of public attitudes toward U.S. business was taken in 1950 by the University of Michigan Survey Research Center. Researchers reported that, at the time, only 10 percent of our population felt that, with respect to "big business activity," "the bad effect outweighed the good."[10] By the 1970s, during which most of our environmental laws and regulations were written, public esteem for business had drastically deteriorated. Pollster Daniel Yankelovich, for example, estimated that, as of 1976, the level of confidence in business had "hovered around 19 percent in the past few years.[11] While I do not wish to stretch the meaning of either of these statistics, it seems perfectly reasonable to conclude that public confidence in business over the period from 1950 to the mid-1970s dropped from around 90 percent approval to nearly 20 percent approval.

Is it sheer coincidence that the environmental laws, which in their mood and application are often inimical to U.S. business interests, were written during the period when public approval of business was at this low ebb? I do not think so. Can we believe that Congress is really so deaf to constituent opinion that the spirit of business criticism evident at the time did not find its way into legislation? I do not think that is the case either.

David Vogel sees this, in part, as a struggle for power between classes in our society:

> ... what is novel about the politics of business–government relations during the past fifteen years [1965-80] is that conflicts over the scope of social regulation have affected directly the power and wealth of the private sector vis-a-vis non–business interest groups. In essence, during the seventies, the controversy over the social regulation of business became the focus of class conflict: it pitted the interests of business as a whole against the public interest movement as well as much of organized labor. The nature of the conflict over regulation became analogous to the struggle over the adoption of the welfare state and the recognition of unions that defined class conflict during the 1930s.[12]

Another political scientist, John Steiner, suggests that conflict such as we have seen is in fact inevitable in a democratic, capitalist society, constituting a "structural adversarial relationship." Steiner reports:

> Capitalist economies and democratic governments differ and there is a natural tension between the two. Democracy is marked by popular sovereignty, political equality and majority rule. The ultimate goal is popular direction of

policy and equality of opportunity and material circumstance. A capitalist system, on the other hand, is marked by a tendency toward accumulation of wealth in the hands of a few and domination by those forces which control the productive processes.[13]

In fact, from the nineteenth century French statesman, de Tocqueville,[14] down to most contemporary economists and political scientists, there has been recognition of the continuing struggle for power in our society, often expressed through class aspirations. The public, however, does not like to use the "class" model in defining power relationships between groups. A more acceptable approach is suggested by economist Arthur Okun when he says that the basic problem inherent in business–government conflict is that of balancing two equally legitimate but variant value systems,[15] which in fact are those mentioned by John Steiner. Thus, these writers feel that continued conflict can be expected between the basic values of capitalism with its free market implications and those other ideals of our society that aspire to political equality and social egalitarianism.

Seen in this light, the best use of consultation, as I am advocating it here, can be to ease the swings of policy from one power center to another, dampening the punitive effects of temporary ascendency of one value system over the other. Specific consultative mechanisms that could bring this about will be examined in later chapters.

No analysis of modern conflict between these values could possibly be complete without mentioning the reemergence of the business lobby in national politics. There has been enormous growth in the quantity and quality of the corporate presence in Washington, D.C., since the advent of the wave of social legislation discussed above.

The perception of these changing power relationships had much to do with the rise of corporate attempts to influence government through increases in traditional activities such as lobbying, as well as through corporate support of political action committees (PACs) in the 1970s and early 1980s. It should be recalled that, during the period between the enactment of New Deal legislation and the beginning of the present epoc of social regulation, business — though always in evidence — played a relatively quiescent role in the enactment of public policy. Chief executives of large corporations seemed to see themselves more as "statesmen" than as political advocates. The reasons for this constitute a story in itself. While motives doubtless ranged over a wide spectrum, one dominant theme was to assert that corporate "good citizenship" required the firm's officers to refrain from controversial statements. Thus, the company's image could be maintained at a "sanitary" level without projecting images that might make potential stockholders or customers nervous. Politics for individuals were encouraged — a mark of good citizenship — but the company must not align itself with any particular ideology or party.

This posture worked fairly well for U.S. business for several decades. It was to be effectively ended by the politicizing of public policy in the social regulation area and by the imposition of the command-and-control philosophy by Congress when it wrote the laws underlying those regulations.

Today the dominant mode of business toward politics is to strongly advocate a position that will advance the interests of an individual firm or at least of the industry in which the firm is positioned. Thus, even among industries dominated by small firms, there are very active industry associations supported by financial contributions from members, thrusting programs and reforms of sundry descriptions at Congress. The National Association of Home Builders and the National Association of Realtors are examples. These groups were enormously energetic in advocating federal monetary policy to improve the lot of their members during the 1980-82 recession.

Larger firms maintain an individual presence in Washington through government affairs departments, which is awesome when measured by former standards. Between 1968 and 1978 the number of corporate public affairs offices in Washington increased from 100 to more than 500.[16] These operations are typically staffed by six or seven people, compared to an anemic cadre of one or two in former periods. When this is added to more than 2,000 trade associations of the type mentioned above, it becomes clear that business is strongly determined to contest those policies that it seems as harmful to business interests and has the people to make its positions heard.

Underscoring all of this is the massive development, since 1974, of corporate political action committees. The number of these entities, about which much has been written lately, has burgeoned from an initial 89 to nearly 1,000 at the time of writing. It has been estimated that by the end of the 1970s corporations were spending close to $900 million yearly on this type of activity (most of it, of course, through contributions by stockholders and employees).[17] Thus, the perceived threat of the very overt political action engaged in throughout the 1970s by advocates of social legislation (most notably that affecting the environment), which has been discussed in Part I of this book, has fostered a very substantial countereffort on the part of business. In a recent survey of corporate executives working in public affairs, 71 percent said that the increase in their companies' involvement in policy issues was due to "the impact of recent government regulations and legislation."[18]

A third, and perhaps dominant, area of influence driving the adversarial relationship can be seen in the legal form that Congress has seen fit to design into social legislation and that the courts have vastly extended through precedent. There are two views on the way that the legal system promotes the adversarial relationship. It would be fair to characterize these as the "intent" school of thought, and the "structure" school.

Typifying the first of these, Michele Corash, the former general counsel of the EPA, believes that Congress's intent was that the statutes should operate in such a way that the various stakeholders in the environment, including government agencies, should not and need not be trusted. She feels that it is "unmistakable" that Congress intended that the various players in the environmental game be adversaries, with all the distrust and lack of cooperation that the role implies.[19] She suggests the following five ways in which the environmental statutes governing actions of the EPA and other agencies promote the adversarial relationship.

Too much specifity. The laws pinpoint as much of the decision making as possible in the statute itself, thus leaving little room for decision making on the part of agencies, industry, public interest groups, or states. The major difficulty with this is that decisions, once incorporated into law, cannot be easily updated in the light of new information, and environmental regulation involves rapidly changing technology as well as shifting social needs and priorities.

Inability to balance competing interests. Government agencies are not allowed to forego short-term benefits as a tradeoff for greater long-term gains. Companies are required to install expensive pollution equipment, often on outdated facilities, which reduces the incentive to replace old equipment with new less polluting plant in the long run. EPA cannot grant the kind of waiver that would allow a planned, long-term solution to pollution problems through new facilities. Again, the Clean Air Act allows the enforcing agency to consider "only health factors" in making regulatory decisions. This is in contrast to British law, which says that the regulating agency must consider economic factors as well as health, thus making possible the often delicate tradeoff between the environment and jobs or investment.

A requirement of perfection. Neither government agencies nor businesses are allowed to risk failure. Alternatives that are known to work must be chosen, even if they do not protect the environment as fully or as efficiently as potential new developments might.

Unrealistic deadlines. Inflexible and unrealistic deadlines written into the law are usually not based on sound technical information, but on hypotheses that frequently cannot be supported in operation. Examples of this can be seen in the auto emissions field, where the original statute target dates for elimination of emissions that were written in the 1970 Clean Air Act were later deemed to be technically and economically unfeasible. In addition to imposing strict requirements of pollution reduction on auto manufacturers, the 1970 law required the EPA to set nationwide air quality standards, and each state had to submit implementation plans to the EPA by mid-1975. On that deadline not one state had complied with the requirement. The statute was amended in 1977.

Another example is the deadlines written into the Clean Water Act. The act disastrously overestimated the ability of chemically related industries to totally eliminate toxic effluents within the economic framework of several industries.[20] The result of this error was a significant amendment of the Clean Water Act to align it with technical reality. While it is possible to amend laws, the seeming requisite that entire industries must be in severe trouble before relief can be dragged from Congress certainly provides a major exacerbation of the relationship between business and government.

Elaborate procedural rules. The rules under which agencies and other stakeholders must operate seem to ignore the original intent of NEPA — the mandate to provide a clean environment without seriously disrupting the social and economic system. These rules, in fact, reward the group that prepares the best position paper for judicial review, not the one that provides the best solutions to problems. They place the emphasis on playing the game, and winning, not on achieving the best results for the environment or the economy.

The other aspect of our environmental laws that has done a great deal to increase the tensions between all parties to environmental decisionmaking is the nature or "structure" of the Administrative Procedures Act (APA), under which virtually all agency decisions wind up being reviewed by the courts. This, together with the progressive broadening of the rules by the courts, permitting "standing" by a wide range of public interest groups,[21] has led many scholars to conclude that the APA now consists of the APA's fairness model modified by a public interest model of proper procedure.[22]

The procedures of the APA work in the following way. Almost all rules promulgated by agencies are done through the "informal rule-making" procedure of the APA. These rules simply require that an agency must publish the rules it proposes to adopt in the Federal Register. After a suitable waiting period for comment from the public, the agency is free to enforce the rules. In the past, agencies were free to consult with any interested parties they chose about the content of rules, both in advance of publication and during the waiting period. In recent years the courts, concerned about how to judge if a rule is fair and reasonable (two of the requirements of the APA), have imposed stricter procedural requirements on the government agencies. These rulings have been described in some detail in Chapter 3. The net effect is to prohibit consultation with interested parties. Most agency counsels are sufficiently concerned about having regulations struck down by the courts that they regularly advise their staff members to avoid such consultation.

Agencies accordingly find themselves issuing regulations in highly technical fields such as hazardous waste disposal without benefit of consultation with industry or public interest experts. Even during the limited period of time allowed for comment by the public, presumably including those very experts, agencies cannot engage in open dialogue with stakeholders to facilitate problem solving.

This "structural" arrangement, then, requires that industry and the public be saddled with regulations that they have barely seen prior to promulgation and for which expert input (outside of that of agency staff experts) has been limited to the writing of a letter that has not even been answered. In the end, if industry does not approve of a new regulation, it must attack the ruling in court. In this arena, managers hardly need to be reminded that the name of the game is not reason, let alone compromise, but to win. Any tactic, including procedural objections over irrelevant details, constitutional objections, delay, or discovery of error on the part of the government agency may be sufficient for industry or public interest groups to block regulation. Judgments are often made <u>not on the merits of the regulation</u>, but on procedural grounds — for now the only way to have your view prevail is to be an <u>adversary</u>.

In sum, then, the adversarial relationship between business and government has been one of long standing. There is a tradition of mutual hostility between these two. Their attitudes have been exacerbated in recent years by the politicizing of social change to affect government policy through the legislature. This is typified by the enactment of rigid laws to control pollution and other social variables.

We have seen that there is some basis for conflict between two desirable values, egalitarianism and freedom to operate in the marketplace. Both provide benefits for our society, but they often occupy opposing roles in the attainment of national goals of democracy and prosperity.

Decline in public esteem for business over the last several decades has contributed to an upper hand for public interest groups in the initiation of social regulation, most notably that affecting the environment. The organization of business to provide offsetting Washington lobbies has added to the hostility between these forces. Finally, the statutes that establish the procedures for regulation making are themselves distrustful, allowing little room for agency application of common sense or compromise. Their prohibitions against consultation lock out environmental stakeholders from the regulation process in such a way that it is necessary to litigate every objection to agency policy.

Surely this system of institutionalized wrangling, which almost forces environmental stakeholders to mistrust and despise one another, is the most procrustean and difficult way to protect the environment. Can we not design better systems to allow the representation of society's interests in the public environmental policy process? Other nations do. I believe that we can.

NOTES

1. One need only turn on the evening news on any national television network to experience the regular use of such terms as "polluter" and "price gouger" in the general case, as though they applied to every business. I can recall only very rare national media questions about the merits of government regulation or for that matter any inference that regulation might be too costly, either in terms of money or restrictions on decision making.

2. See, for example, George Mowry, _Theodore Roosevelt and the Progressive Movement_ (New York: Hill and Wang, 1946).

3. See, for example, Herbert Shapiro, ed., _The Muckrakers and American Society_ (Boston: D.C. Heath, 1968).

4. David Vogel, "The New Social Regulation in Historical and Comparative Perspective," in _Regulation in Perspective_, ed. Thomas K. McCraw (Boston: Harvard Business School, 1981).

5. Ibid., pp. 157-59.

6. See George A. Steiner, "An Overview of the Changing Business Environment and Its Impact on Business," paper delivered at a conference concerned with business environment/public policy, July 8-13, 1979, Washington University, St. Louis, p. 10.

7. See also Charles L. Schultz, _The Public Use of Private Interest_ (Washington, D.C.: Brookings Institution, 1977).

8. Organization for Economic Cooperation and Development, _Environmental Policies in Japan_ (Paris: OECD, 1977), p. 33.

9. Ibid., p. 23.

10. In Burton R. Fisher and Stephen B. Withey, _Big Business As the People See It: A Study of a Socio-Economic Institution_, University Microfilms, Ann Arbor, 1951, p. xii.

11. Daniel Yankelovich, speech before the UCLA Graduate School of Management.

12. Vogel, "New Social Regulation," p. 165.

13. John F. Steiner, "Cynicism Toward Big Business in America: An Analysis of Underlying Causal Factors," paper of the Center for Research and Dialogue on Business and Society, UCLA, Los Angeles, 1976, p. 7.

14. Alexis de Tocqueville, _Democracy in America_, ed. Richard Heffner (New York: New American Library, 1956), p. 219.

15. Arthur Okun, _Equality and Efficiency: The Big Trade-Off_ (Washington, D.C.: Brookings Institution, 1976).

16. "Washington's Big Boom," _Duns Review_ (July 1978):51.

17. Neil Ulman, "Companies Organize Employees and Holders into a Political Force," _Wall Street Journal_ (August 15, 1978):1-15.

18. Phyllis McGrath, "Redefining Corporate-Federal Regulations," _Conference Board Report No. 757_, 1979.

19. Michele B. Corash, "Governmental Regulation: A Consensual Alternative," in _Corporations and the Environment: How Should Decisions Be Made?_, Graduate School of Business, Stanford University, 1981, p. 59.

20. Robert A. Leone, _Environmental Controls_ (Boston: Lexington Books, 1976).

21. Karen Orren, "Standing to Sue," _American Political Science Review_ 70 (September 1976):724.

22. See, for example, American Bar Association Commission on Law and the Economy, _Federal Regulation: Roads to Reform_ (Washington, D.C.: 1978).

6
The Environment and the Reagan Administration

There has been a temptation among administration watchers to spin out scenarios about the values and attitudes of the Reagan administration toward the environment. Issues of environmental protection have been in the news frequently enough to encourage a variety of story lines, all attempting to explain the relationship between the motivations of the administration and the results seen in the media. The public is concerned about the problems of toxic waste, acid rain, and the recent mismanagement of the EPA. These issues and others have fostered considerable speculation about the administration's goals and motivation.

Writers have depicted the "true role" of the administration in environmental protection as being at both ends of the spectrum of support for regulation. The comments of Rita Lavelle, in an internal memo she allegedly wrote to her boss prior to her dismissal in February 1983, sent environmental writers scurrying for their strongest pejoratives. The memo characterized EPA General Counsel Robert Perry as "systematically alienating the primary constituents of this administration, the business community." The revelations of that period about the management of EPA coupled with the substantial reductions in budget and staff effected by the administrator, Anne Gorsuch (who has more recently become Anne Burford), were enough to spark allegations that the administration was intentionally trying to "dismantle" the EPA and put an end to environmental protection.

On the other hand, many defended the actions at EPA and in James Watt's Interior Department as a "rationalization" of overgrown bureaucracy and a recognition that, like anything else, we must pay for the environmental protection we get, and we ought to be prudent in that expenditure. The latter view hews most closely to the publicized administration line.

It is my opinion that the truth lies neither with nor between these extremes of thought, but along another dimension altogether. It is easy when analyzing issues with political overtones to fall into the trap of assuming the validity of the nostrum that says, "you're either with us or against us." While this kind of unidimensional analysis may be useful in polarizing and simplifying issues during a political campaign, I doubt its utility in analyzing issues of public policy.

I would like, then, to suggest another way of looking at the administration's posture toward environmental protection and then provide some evidence for my views. To explain these views, a few factors will be discussed that have had a critical influence on the value patterns of the administration: the priorities of the administration, the changing public mood toward the environment since the president was elected, and budgetary pressures.

THE PRIORITIES OF THE ADMINISTRATION

Clearly, the high-priority issues for the president and his administration are a revitalization of the economy and an improvement in our national defense posture. An important corollary for the administration is an effort to reduce the size of government. The first two of these have been the subject of massive legislative efforts, and as this is written, though the president's legislative program for the economy is largely in place, future annual defense appropriations for the increased growth in the armed forces demanded by the president are still subject to debate.

These priorities relate to environmental protection in two very important ways. First, the administration is preoccupied at both the administrative- and legislative-relations levels with what are seen as more urgent concerns. There is just not time and energy available to deal with environmental policy. Hence, it is relegated to agency administrators who are allowed to operate with minimal oversight from the White House. Second, there is not sufficient political capital available for the president to be willing to spend any on the environment. The administration may wish to improve the regulatory process in a variety of ways: to make it more responsive to the environmental stakeholders, to reduce the difficult bureaucratic red tape associated with regulation, or to pursue myriad other interests. The facts are that while its legislative program has been bound up with the controversial and difficult to achieve economic and defense legislation that the president desires, the administration has chosen to use virtually all of its influence on those issues.

In an article written about the time President Reagan was inaugurated,[1] I predicted that his administration would limit its action in relation to the environment to administrative changes within agencies and to moderate revisions of environmental laws, if any were proposed. This seems to have occurred. While my analysis mainly considered the strength of environmental issues within Congress, and among the public, the priorities of the administration, as well as recognition of that strength, have certainly dictated that energy and influence not be expended in the environmental direction.

The effort to reduce the size of government has been a concern of the president's throughout his political career. It has affected environmental processes by pressuring agencies to reduce staff and cut their budgets in other ways. It has provided the philosophical strength to enable administrators, particularly new political appointees, to design budgets in a manner most contrary to usual bureaucratic motivation. Reagan did, after all, prior to his election, promise to "get the government off of the backs of business."

THE CHANGING MOOD OF THE PUBLIC

When the Reagan administration took office in January 1981, support for environmental regulation had moved from being perceived as a crisis, as described in previous chapters, to a considerably less critical issue. At the same time there was concern that the costs of regulation might be too high for the economy to afford, and in some quarters, particularly the most conservative, there was an expectation that the Reagan administration would bring about drastic reductions in regulation.

Earlier chapters have demonstrated that there continued to be strong support for environmental protection, and some evidence of environmental concern in that period was provided. A Harris Poll commissioned by _Business Week_, conducted early in January 1983, provides insight into the shifting mood about the environment between 1981 and 1983.[2] The poll, when compared with results of a similar poll in 1981, shows that while there was definite concern in 1981 about whether we had gone too far with environmental regulation, a remarkable reversal has taken place since that time. The following figures compare public opinion in the two periods.

Support for a stronger Clean Air Act has risen from 29 to 47 percent over the period. Support for stronger clean water laws has gone up from 52 to 61 percent over the same time. Those interviewed favoring _less_ stringent air regulations dropped from 17 to 7 percent. The relaxation of auto pollution standards was favored by 38 percent of those polled in 1981. This approval has dropped to 26 percent. Willingness to ease air standards to allow burning of high-sulfur coal in power plants has dropped from 29 to 19 percent. The public's strongest concerns seem to be reserved for the control of hazardous waste disposal and toxic pollution of lakes and rivers. Respectively, 86 and 88 percent opposed weakening these regulations.

Harris probed further, asking respondents whether they could justify the weakening of environmental laws for any reason. In one example of questioning, they were asked if a factory whose pollutants were dangerous to human health should be granted relief from standards. Reasons suggested included the supposition that the factory would shut down and jobs lost if relief were not given. Respondents were adamant, with 78 percent holding that no reason whatsoever is sufficient to relax standards in that situation.

Harris attributes the dramatic shift in opinion to "the intervention of a political event." He says that citizens became deeply concerned about their perception that Interior Secretary James Watt and EPA Administrator Anne Gorsuch were hostile to the laws they were charged with enforcing. Significantly, 55 percent of the sample believed that environmental organizations were doing a good job in trying to get standards enforced.

BUDGETARY PRESSURES

Ronald Reagan's penchant for reducing the size of government has been evident throughout his political life. Nowhere has its influence been more evident than in the recent enforcement of environmental regulation. There are, however, two aspects to the pressure on agency heads throughout the federal government to reduce expenditures. This general entreaty for economy is certainly transmitted through the Office of Management and Budget to all agencies; in addition, however, the rising defense budget and corresponding huge federal deficits have encouraged a drastic look at expenditures in all nonentitlement areas, most particularly the social expenditures of government.

In this environment, agency administrators, such as Gorsuch, have simply looked at budget cuts as practicing compliance with administration policy. Nor could the president, after exhortations to economize, refuse budget reductions, regardless of the personal motivations of the managers in the agency.

It may be, as Lou Harris says the public believes, that Gorsuch, Watt, and others are actually hostile to their regulatory duties, but even if that is so, there is every opportunity provided by the budget constraints as well to economize on regulatory functions. It must be emphasized that there is a vast difference between reductions aimed deliberately at the crippling of an agency and a desire to administer more efficiently. Members of the public may have decided where the truth lies on the hostility issue. However, I have not seen enough evidence to convince me, one way or the other.

The numbers, however, are impressive. For example, when the president was inaugurated, there were over 14,000 people working at EPA. The Gorsuch budget for 1983 provided for 10,396 positions. Hazardous waste personnel dropped from 311 in 1981 to 75 in 1983. That administrative budget dropped from $11.4 million to $2.3 million. The proposed budget for grants to states to help clean up hazardous wastes in 1984 cut those grants 26 percent, from $233 million to $172 million. Clearly, budget pressures have been at work.

It is not surprising either that morale was at an all time low at EPA in the early months of 1983. Anne Gorsuch, who had been labeled early on as the "ice queen" because of her cold demeanor, was acknowledged, off the record, to be a poor manager by members of the administration. This, coupled with massive staff reductions and the inevitable uncertainty of the remaining employees about the security of their jobs, provided a predictable formula for chaos in the agency. Voltair remarked, referring to the French bureaucracy, "When there is mischief at the top, there is misery at the bottom." While I am not willing to impute culpability to the EPA management, the effect certainly seems to have been the same.

It seems highly probable to me, then, that what has transpired on the Reagan environmental record is largely the result of a set of priorities that superseded environmental issues, coupled with rigid budget constraints. The public outcry about the Reagan environmental record is entirely consistent with the position I have insisted on throughout this book: namely, that there is and has been for many years a very strong value in the United States for environmental protection. It never went away. It merely went underground. When the public became concerned about inflation and unemployment as critical issues, in the late 1970s and early 1980s, these issues superseded the environment. However, the ongoing attitude of James Watt, and the crisis at EPA in early 1983, have provided environmentalists with sufficient ammunition to convince many people that they need to reassert their interest in the environment. Subsequent events have shown that the administration understands this and has moved to reestablish both competence and confidence at EPA. James Watt's Interior Department remains another matter.

A review of the Reagan administration's management of its environmental functions should add substance to my assertions. First, we will look at the EPA.

It was not until mid-February 1983 that the public became aware that there were serious problems at EPA. While Administrator Anne Gorsuch had previously been referred to in the press as "the ice queen," a pejorative attached by some workers at the agency to describe her management style, and while there was concern on Capitol Hill about the handling of the $1.6 billion hazardous waste "superfund," most of the agency's problems had been kept in-house. Gorsuch had refused in the previous December to turn over to Congress subpoenaed documents relating to 160 hazardous sites and was cited for contempt of Congress for her obstinacy. She was supported by the president, however, and most people saw the issues as another round in battle between Congress and the administration for dominance in agency oversight.

Then in February the administration itself took a hand in the hazardous waste dispute — the president firing Rita Lavelle, who headed the waste program, and thus providing confirmation of disturbing management problems at the agency. Though there were allegations of criminal activity involved with "sweetheart" deals between Lavelle and some companies who were supposed to be regulated by EPA, as well as ongoing investigations by no less than six congressional subcommittees, there has been, to the date of this writing, no concrete evidence of such duplicity. Rita Lavelle has been convicted for contempt of Congress, while the charges against Anne Gorsuch have been dropped following the president's agreement to provide investigating committees with the documentation they had requested.

While morale at the agency had been very low for some time, the shoal on which Gorsuch's administration was to founder was the management of the hazardous waste "superfund." Rita Lavelle is a former employee of the California chemical company, Aerojet General Corporation. She agreed at her confirmation hearings in February 1982 to excuse herself from any deliberations involving that company. According to Newsweek, many EPA insiders say she did not. Lavelle did not make herself popular when she began announcing that she had a special relationship with White House Counselor Edwin Meese (a friendship denied by Meese). She referred to Meese as her "godfather." According to one former EPA official, "She came into the agency like a Mack truck. . . . She simply wasn't suited for a position at that level."[3] Democrats in the House charged that Lavelle was responsible for holding up funds for the cleanup of the String-fellow Acid Pits near Riverside, California, to prevent California ex-Governor Jerry Brown from claiming a cleanup to his benefit in his campaign for the Senate. Lavelle denied this. She feuded with EPA General Counsel Robert Perry over the String-fellow issue, and it was on this account that she wrote the memo about Perry referred to earlier. On top of this, in December Lavelle had clashed with the House Subcommittee on Science and Technology over allegations that she had asked the EPA inspector general to investigate Hugh Kaufman, an EPA employee and whistle blower who had criticized management of the superfund.

Subcommittee Chairman James H. Scheuer produced evidence to the contrary and announced that he was ready to ask the Justice Department to prosecute Lavelle for perjury. While the issue was never pressed, Scheuer says, "They dumped her because she got caught in perjury."4

By late February, the lid was off at the agency, and allegations were flying thick and fast. Matthew Novick, the EPA inspector general, who would himself be asked to resign days later, released a report suggesting that more than $53 million of superfund monies may have been used for unauthorized agency purposes and charged to the superfund account. Representative Scheuer commented that "at best, EPA officials have been sloppy and incompetent. . . . At worst, they may have knowingly looted Superfund." He called the administration at the EPA "unprofessional, unbelievably amateurish and incompetent management."5

Congressional subcommittees were by now leaking all manner of charges about how the EPA handled the people's business. Some of them were petty, some potentially important, but all of them lent strength to the impression of massive mismanagement at the agency, if not downright improper behavior. The White House ordered a Justice Department investigation to ferret out any wrongdoing and then agreed to release the superfund documents Congress had requested.

In March the polls began to reflect a significant increase in the number of people who felt the president's policies were damaging to the environment. Republicans in Congress began to call for the resignation of Gorsuch (now Anne Burford). The White House held firm for a while, but as more charges began to pile up the president "allowed" Anne Burford to resign. Reagan emphasized that the resignation was her decision alone and that he had not requested it. Two Republican Representatives, James Jeffords of Vermont and Claudine Schneider of Rhode Island, had summed it all up in a letter to colleagues a few days before: "It is not in the best interests of the Republican Party for the credibility of the EPA's commitment to environment protection to remain in doubt." The president had received the message.

What followed seemed almost an anticlimax, as the professionals in the White House began to reweave the strands of EPA credibility. Almost a dozen high-level resignations were asked for and received. A search seemed to have been underway for some time for a replacement for Burford as EPA administrator. Within 12 days of Burford's resignation, the president named William Ruckelshaus as the new administrator. Ruckelshaus has a strong following among environmentalists. He was the first administrator of the EPA and is credited with setting the agency up in a responsible and initially noncontroversial way. Above all, he has a reputation for integrity and good management, having been fired at the Justice Department's "Saturday night massacre" for refusing to fire Watergate Special Prosecutor Archibald Cox. His return to government from a post as a vice-president of Weyerhaeuser, the forest products company, was hailed within and without the EPA as a good start. He was confirmed by the Senate without a single dissenting vote. At the agency he was greeted as a returning hero, with members of the staff hoisting a banner that read: "How Do You Spell Relief? Ruckelshaus."

James Watt, the former secretary of the interior, was a highly controversial figure beginning with his confirmation by the Senate at the start of the Reagan administration. His departure from the Reagan cabinet in October 1983 was the consequence of the twin problems of his environmental policies and his tart-tongued insensitivity in public utterances. Environmentalists were enraged by his bold attempts to push development of public lands, but the critical incident of his demise was his remark about the composition of a coal-leasing advisory commission. His statement about the makeup of the group including blacks, women, Jews, and a cripple was taken by Republicans as the last straw in a string of public gaffes considered too insensitive for a high-level official.

Watt's career was indeed controversial. He spearheaded an administration drive to exploit resources on public lands and under the continental shelves as a partial remedy for energy problems. In this role, he announced plans to lease almost one billion acres of the continental shelf for oil drilling by 1987. Coal policy, too, under Watt revolved around the sale or leasing of public lands to allow for the development of energy sources. The most recent of the sales of public lands, which were so controversial among environmentalists, was the auction of 450 million acres on the North Dakota-Montana border. Watt pushed this through in spite of strenuous protest by the House Interior Committee and a suit by two environmental groups.

For his part, Watt maintains that, without considering development policy, the management of public lands had never been better, and he should be praised for outstanding management. He developed a series of statistics and charts to show that the Interior Department, under his administration, increased spending on maintenance of national parks and enlarged the number of recovery plans for endangered species. Environmentalists refused to believe any of it. According to Jay D. Hair, executive vice-president of the conservative National Wildlife Federation, Watt is a "radical ideologue." He said, "I don't know where he gets his numbers, but they are not the same numbers everyone else has."[6] Various influential Republicans had seen Watt as a political problem; in fact, Republican National Committee Chairman Frank J. Fahrenkopf was quoted in the <u>Los Angeles Times</u> fairly early in Watt's tenure saying that Watt was a "liability."

The battle over Watt existed, however, on at least two levels. There is truly a difference in the outlook about the U.S. political process on the part of Watt and most of his critics. Here is a sample of vintage Watt on the subject of social policy:

I believe we are battling for the form of government under which we and future generations will live. . . . That's the battle. The battle's not over the environment. If it was, they [the environmentalists] would be with us. They want to control social behavior and conduct.[7]

He said environmentalists

. . . are obviously not [interested in the environment]. . . . Their agenda is hard line partisan politics. They want social behavior controlled [from Washington]. That's what drives me. That's why I'll never give up. We will pursue this crusade as long as there is breath in our being.[8]

Environmentalists, of course, attacked Watt with equal fury. Cecil Andrus, secretary of the interior under President Carter said, "He's a failure because he cannot or does not accept or even understand the trust or stewardship of the nation's resources."

While Watt, a master polemist, substantially overstated his case and while there certainly were environmental issues involved in the dispute between the secretary and the nation's environmentalists, there may well have been a substantial degree of truth present in his analysis. It seems to me that, at root, we are dealing with the same dichotomy of values, both important to our society, first delineated by de Tocqueville in the early nineteenth century and recognized down through the decades by political scientists and economists as powerful formers of our national character — the twin desires for freedom of enterprise and an egalitarian society. These equally important values have been mentioned in the previous chapter. With his passionate defense of free enterprise and his identification with the business interest in resource development, Watt signaled to environmentalists that his priorities would lie with the free enterprise value whenever conflict arose between the two. For their part, most environmental groups are publicly committed to a "sharing" of the nation's resources among all of the people.

Thus, it may well be that the president valued Watt more for his willingness to stand for what Reagan sees as vital U.S. attributes than for his environmental policies. It was also suggested that Watt was a useful lightning rod to draw environmental wrath away from the president. As one White House staff member put it, "The environmental groups need a target. If they didn't have Jim, they'd have to invent him." Watt's departure from the administration should thus be seen as recognition of the political power of environmentalists as much as concern about the man's public utterances.

In summary, I do not believe that it is accurate to charge that the Reagan administration is insensitive to the environment. Sensitivity is a matter of degree. All humans maintain a hierarchy of values, in which many things are considered valuable, but some hold priority over others. I think it _is_ clear that the administration has priorities that it holds higher than its concerns about environmental protection, namely, the economy and national defense. These priorities and the budget constraints invoked by them, as well as the president's concern about making government smaller, have weakened the agencies responsible for protecting the environment — although some would say that the weakening was more a problem of morale than of function.

That the administration is sensitive to the _political_ reality of supporting environmental issues is readily apparent from its actions at the EPA when the White House finally became convinced that the electorate perceived substantial mismanagement there. Reagan's employment of James Watt seems to me to have been more in support of Watt's outspoken free-enterprise values than of his environmental views.

Attacks on the president as the "destroyer of the environment" seem as overdrawn as Watt's broadsides at environmentalists. It is worth noting that the Harris survey referred to before shows that slightly more Republicans than Democrats claim membership in and financial support of environmental groups (13 to 10 percent) and that Reagan has been careful to attack only those whom he defines as "environmental extremists." It may also be useful to recall the advice of activist William L. Brian, which was quoted in Chapter 3:

> Once the environmentalist has set overall humanitarian goals, he should follow the strategies of successful political activists, such as choosing a popular issue, building grassroots support, timing, crisis precipitation, flexibility, and openness to legal aid or negotiation.[9]

If this sounds a lot like what environmental groups are doing, perhaps it is because the kind of tactics that Brian recommends have become accepted ways of achieving results in the political arena. There is no reason why the environmental movement should not emulate that example. It does mean, however, that we can expect environmental groups to continue to attack the administration and to use circumstances that really represent an expression of differences in values in an attempt to foster a perception of crisis wherever possible.

NOTES

1. C. Wesley Morse, "Environmental Regulation in the United States: The Coming Changes," _Journal of General Management_ 6 (Spring 1981):62-71.
2. Louis Harris and Associates, _Business Week_, January 24, 1983, p. 67.
3. Quoted in _Time_, February 21, 1983, p. 14.
4. Ibid., p. 15.
5. _Newsweek_, February 28, 1983, pp. 14-15.
6. Quoted in _Newsweek_, April 11, 1983, p. 35.
7. Quoted in _International Herald Tribune_, May 5, 1983, p. 6.
8. Quoted in _Newsweek_, April 11, 1983, p. 35.
9. William L. Bryant, "Toward a Viable Environmental Movement," _Journal of Applied Behavioral Science_ 10 (March 1974):387.

7
Consultation

Consultation plays an important role in the regulatory process throughout most of the industrial world. Governments rely on an interchange of ideas with industry and other environmental stakeholders at many levels. Thus, the Japanese emphasis on harmonizing national goals with local needs provides one perspective, emphasizing the potential for direct discussions between industry and government. The European penchant for "rationalizing" national regulatory differences through the European Economic Community (EEC) and its Commission of the European Communities provides insight into consultation at the macropolicy level.

This chapter will examine the British system of environmental regulation, one that is unique within the European community and brings the practice of consultation to a broader spectrum of regulatory activity than any other. Because of this and because of the many cultural similarities between policy formation in the United States and Britain, I conducted in 1981 a comprehensive study of British environmental regulation. Parts of the study that compare regulation making and administration in the two countries will be presented in this chapter.

Though we are principally interested in consultation, it is desirable for at least two reasons to look at the whole sweep of environmental regulation. First, we need to see how consultation

---

Portions of this chapter have appeared in C. Wesley Morse, "Environmental Regulation for the Future: Some Lessons from British Policy," _California Management Review_ 26 (Fall 1983): 25-36. Copyright @ 1983 by the Regents of the University of California. Reprinted by permission of the Regents.

varies throughout the system and, second, the practice is so pervasive in Britain that we must examine the system as a whole to see consultation as the sum of its parts.

The research project included interviews with scores of managers in several of Britain's largest enterprises, both privately and government owned. It also involved interviews with executives in government agencies, with environmentalists, and with academics.[1] The data collected highlighted three substantial differences between U.S. environmental regulation and that of Great Britain:[2] the form of the law, the nature of regulations issued under laws, and the process of consultation.

THE FORM OF THE LAW

A significant feature of U.S. environmental law, as it is worked out in practice, is the apparent ease with which stakeholders can get access to the courts. Court challenges sometimes tie up major projects for years, while jurists slowly work their way through caseloads and complex legal procedures.

Most readers are familiar with a number of sizable projects that have been greatly changed or cancelled due to these delays. A few of these were the Dow petrochemical project in California, cancelled in 1977; the famous snail darter episode regarding Tellico Dam on the Little Tennessee River, where construction was halted in 1977; the Sohio Long Beach, California, pipeline project, cancelled in 1979; and the Northern Tier pipeline project at Port Angeles, Washington, cancelled in 1982.

Most managers feel that the practice of opposing large industrial developments through court action has become standard procedure for environmental groups and local special interests. As a permanent fixture of the process of obtaining government approval for environmentally sensitive projects, referral to the courts for final decisions is seen by many as expensive, inefficient, and time consuming.

Under the British system, on the other hand, only unusual circumstances qualify for access to the courts. All appeals from regulatory decisions must be made to the ministry responsible for the administration of the law. In such appeals the decision of the minister is final. The system works in the following way: Statutes are assigned to particular ministries for administration. Each ministry (department of government) is headed by a secretary of state (minister) appointed by the prime minister for the period of the prime minister's tenure in office, or at the behest of the prime minister. Departments are permanently administered by a staff of civil servants who tend to remain in employment regardless of the political party in power.

Issues of regulation may be referred to the High Court if the minister chooses to define a "special case" turning on a question of law. In such a case, the minister will be bound by the decision of the court. Local authorities (town councils and so on) may bring a "nuisance action" in the courts against industry in cases of excess pollution, but again, only with the <u>consent of the minister</u>. Except for these two special circumstances, final appeal is to the department responsible for administration, and the decision of the appropriate minister is thus final.[3]

British managers who were interviewed were aware of the workings of this system. They tended to use a planning strategy involving consultation with civil servants in appropriate departments at the outline stage of projects. They negotiated to obtain agreement on critical planning details and were thus able to take the department's view into account early in the project. Hence, government censure at later, more costly stages was avoided.

THE NATURE OF REGULATIONS

In the United States, regulatory agencies rely heavily on "fixed emission standards." This approach attempts to ensure that any pollution source, wherever in the country, will be limited to a certain maximum quantity of pollutants. Fixed emission standards are applied to both air and water sources. There has recently been evidence that the Environmental Protection Agency will, in some circumstances, consider regional air quality in assessing specific projects (to be discussed in greater detail later). Still, the dominant policy continues to adhere to fixed emission standards.

In Britain major air pollution sources (those in such industries as lead, iron and steel, petroleum refineries, electricity and gas works, cement manufacturing, and most chemical processes) are regulated through operations of the Alkali Inspectorate. Minor sources of air pollution are treated by nuisance legislation and will not be dealt with here. Water quality is controlled by several water authorities on a regional basis. The approach to air and water pollution regulation by these agencies differs considerably and is worthy of discussion.

Air Pollution

Emissions to the air, regulated by the Alkali Inspectorate, are controlled on a case-by-case basis, and while each specific installation is assigned emission limits by the Alkali Inspectorate, <u>environmental quality</u> in the immediate vicinity of the installation is the base criterion. Regional alkali inspectors, in consultation with the managers of individual plants, establish the operating requirements for all operations under their jurisdiction. In doing so, the law requires that they take into account the "best practicable means" and that they express maximum allowable emissions as "presumptive limits."

The Alkali Inspectorate has defined "practicable" as: reasonably practicable, having regard, among other things, to local conditions and circumstances, to the financial implications, and to the current state of technical knowledge. "Means" has been defined as: design, installation, maintenance, manner, and periods of operation of plant and machinery, and the design, construction, and maintenance of buildings. The Alkali Inspectorate's criteria for "presumptive limits" are:

1. No emission can be tolerated that constitutes a demonstrable health hazard, either short or long term.
2. Emissions, in terms of both concentration and mass, must be reduced to the lowest practicable amount.
3. Having secured the minimum practicable emission the height of discharge must be arranged so that emission is rendered harmless and inoffensive. (For highly toxic metals, the concentration of each source to the existing background concentration shall not exceed one-fortieth of the threshold limit value for a factory atmosphere on three-minute mean basis. In deciding on the most important parameter, the effects on vegetation, animals, and amenity are also considered.)

Appeal from the decisions of the regional inspectors may be made to their superiors in the Health and Safety Executive, or in extreme cases, a public hearing may be requested. If a hearing is requested, the minister of the department will decide if issues of sufficient public import are involved to justify a hearing. If a public hearing is granted, a hearing officer will be appointed by the ministry and empowered to make recommendations to the minister, subsequent to the conduct of the hearing. In the case of either a direct appeal or a public hearing, the final decision will be made by the minister. No further appeal is allowed.

The British definition of "best practicable means" includes financial implications as well as technical feasibility. To clarify this, the Alkali Inspectorate has ruled that "the technically possible would be impracticable if the costs were so high that the manufacturing operation were thereby rendered unprofitable or nearly so."[4] When I discussed this use of financial criteria with business executives and civil servants, I was told that the inclusion of costs was necessary to ensure "value for money" for the society as a whole. Decisionmakers are very much concerned about the linkage between profitability and continued employment. This is particularly true in the country's mature industries, such as steel, coal, and railroads.

Thus, the British system allows for the regional variation of emissions and for a consideration of the costs of emission control in the government-industry consultative process. Ultimately, this process determines the exact nature of specific air pollution control standards.

In contrast, the U.S. Environmental Protection Agency is required by the Clean Air Act to base its fixed emission standards "solely on health criteria."

Water Pollution

Liquid effluent standards in Britain are set by regional water authorities. There are ten such bodies, roughly corresponding geographically to the major river systems of the country. Water authorities are responsible for the total management of water in their respective areas of jurisdiction; that is, they control both water supply and disposal. Their activities are coordinated by a statutory body, the National Water Council.

Individual point course pollution limits are established on a case-by-case basis for each industrial or municipal applicant. The basis for establishing limits is the "quality objective" of the receiving body of water. Quality objectives are established by regional water authorities in consultation with local government and industry and relate to the expected use of the water, such as sewerage, recreational, potable, navigational, and so on. Point source limits are set so that the receiving body of water will not be degraded below its established quality objective. The limits of pollution discharge are specified in "consents" or permits, which are renewable every two years.

Technical requirements corresponding to specific quality objectives are established by the National Water Council and expressed as "suggested classifications of river quality."

Water quality is monitored continuously by regional authorities and periodically by the national government. River pollution surveys are carried out every five years by the Department of Environment, and there exists a "Harmonized Monitoring Scheme," managed by the Department of Environment, which collects data annually to maintain a computer data base on water quality throughout the country.

Thus, a particular disposer will not be allowed to discharge effluent into any given body of water if the responsible water authority maintains that the effluent will degrade the specified quality of that particular receiver. Appeal from water authority decisions may be made to the Ministry of the Environment (responsible for water authorities), and the review process is much the same as in air quality regulation discussed above.

Managers I have interviewed were very conscious of the regional nature of British regulation. Local managers were aware of the need to relate to their regional government counterparts in a sophisticated fashion and to develop an ongoing working relationship with these regulators. Most were satisfied that they were treated fairly and that they dealt with individuals that they could respect as experts in their respective technical fields. While it was clearly understood by all parties that regional government employees would always make the final regulatory decision (subject only to appeals), managers were quick to describe the problem-solving nature that was characteristic of the relations between themselves and their government counterparts. In the words of one executive:

> The important thing to remember about our regional Alkali Inspectors is that we are dealing with men who are among the best technically in their field. They are qualified to understand our processes and to make intelligent suggestions to improve our pollution performance. They talk the same technical language as our own engineers, have their respect, command attention and are taken quite seriously. We work closely with them both in the design of new facilities, and in the improvement of older installations. We do so because we must, but also because we value their counsel.

Each of the firms in this study also maintained an environmental staff at the corporate level to provide analysis and advice to regional managers as well as to consult with national authorities and coordinate overall policy.

THE PROCESS OF CONSULTATION

Underlying all environmental regulation in Britain is the process of consultation, which in my opinion is the most important difference between U.S. and British regulation. Consultation between parties involved with regulation is pervasive. Government ministers and civil servants are required by law to consult with a wide variety of stakeholders before making decisions affecting the environment. The environmental laws themselves, as well as regulations effectuating those laws, are framed through an exhaustive process with constituents at a variety of levels of society. A number of standing advisory boards, or consultative groups, advise both ministers and civil servants in the formulation of environmental decisions.

Proposals for new regulations are circulated widely, in confidence, among industry associations, trade union associations, and academic specialists who have a particular competence or an economic interest in the regulations. An underlying philosophy of regulation is cost effectiveness. Economic variables such as productivity, investment, and employment are thus considered along with technical and public health factors in framing and implementing. Consultation is seen by all parties as a valuable tool in harnessing a variety of expertise and interests.

Confidentiality is a fundamental tenet of consultation. Both custom and the law itself require that information given for the purpose of framing or administering environmental laws cannot be released without the permission of the person who is the source of that information. For example, the Health and Safety at Work, etc. Act of 1974 (which also regulates "dangerous substances and certain emissions into the atmosphere") specifies "no relevant information shall be disclosed without the consent of the person by whom it was furnished." Civil servants interviewed during this research stated emphatically that, not only as a matter of law but "as a matter of common sense," information obtained in the course of discussions with consultants or members of the wider public must of necessity remain in confidence. I was told by one senior civil servant charged with environmental policy:

> The value of confidentiality is that it opens up the channels of communication between government, industry, and others affected by legislation. It removes decision-making from the political arena, where it might otherwise be, and it ensures the cooperation of many who might otherwise balk. Confidentiality is truly vital to the operation of this department.

I have said that we need to consider ways in which the EPA and other U.S. agencies can use the resources of industry, and environmentalists, in the protection of the environment. I believe that consultation can provide such an avenue. It was with this in mind that I asked Mike Flux, chief environmental consultant for Britain's giant conglomerate, Imperial Chemical Industries Limited (ICI), a very specific question: "What role did you personally, as well as ICI, play in the preparation of the consultative document, 'Notification of New Substances,' just published by the government's Health and Safety Executive?" This was the draft regulation for control of toxic chemical substances, the counterpart of our Hazardous Waste Regulations, and considered the most important environmental regulation published in Britain in a decade.[5]

Without hesitation, Flux extracted from a file in his desk three copies of the document in question, each about 100 pages in length. "These are successive drafts of the regulation in which you are interested," he said. "The last one here is the draft which was just published. The previous drafts were developed over a period of two years through consultation between business, trade unions, and the Health and Safety Executive." He explained that, as a representative of ICI, he was a member of the Committee on Dangerous Substances of each of two trade associations. These were the Chemical Industries Association (confusingly called the CIA) and the Confederation of British Industry (CBI). In that membership capacity, he was consulted by the Health and Safety Executive (HSE) in the preparation of the successive documents. He described the consultation as "both formal and informal," sometimes difficult, often "hard nosed" (a peculiarly U.S. expression) but conducted with the complete understanding that the regulators at the Health and Safety Executive would always have the last word. He said that in this respect "there is an implied contract in this consulting — you are doing no more than exchanging ideas on a subject. If you break that contract, you have no influence. There is mutual pride in an independent civil service — a belief that there is no untoward influence."

Flux explained further that, following the initial draft of the regulations proposed by HSE, a series of meetings as well as private consultations and comments produced the successive drafts. Each was modified in turn until there was general satisfaction among many conferees with a final document. "One we could all support."

HSE officials confirmed the consultation process described by Flux and added some interesting details of their own: this regulation-making group maintains seven standing advisory committees, each made up of 12 to 24 members drawn from a variety of pertinent professions. Members are selected for technical competence; however, they also represent a cross-section of environmental stakeholders. The committees are:

Advisory Committee on Major Hazards
Advisory Committee on Asbestos
Medical Advisory Committee
Advisory Committee on Dangerous Substances
Advisory Committee on Toxic Substances
Agriculture Industry Advisory Committee
Health and Safety Executive/Local Authority
Liaison Committee*

When the HSE staff members undertake a regulation, they first consult with the appropriate standing advisory committee for the technical area involved. In the case of the "Notification of

---

*"Local Authority" refers to all levels of local government.

New Substances," this was the Advisory Committee on Toxic Substances. The list of members of that committee, as shown in Appendix Table 7.1, will provide an example of the breadth of stakeholder participation at this early stage of consultation.

Beyond the advisory committee, rule makers at HSE are required to consult both formally and informally with a number of bodies. The <u>HSE Guide to Regulation Making Procedure</u> requires the preparation of a "Formal Consultation List" for each regulation proposed. The list must include the following:

- CBI and a suggested list of CBI member organizations with a particular interest in the proposed regulations or code of practice;
- Trades Union Congress (TUC), similarly as in CBI above;
- government departments;
- other government organizations, for example, UKAEA;
- local authority associations;
- employers' and trade association — non-CBI membership;
- trade unions and other work organizations not affiliated to TUC; and
- other bodies.

The <u>HSE Guide</u> states, "as a rough indication, consultation lists will normally comprise about 20 to 40 bodies." The procedure indicates that individual companies will be included on the consultation list "only very rarely, such as . . . when there is no appropriate industry body." Individual persons are "normally never" included in the list.

Thus, the Health and Safety Executive relies heavily on consultation through organized associations of various aspects of British society. These organizations, in turn, appoint knowledgeable individuals to represent the point of view of their group. Business is generally included through appropriate committees of the CBI. Individuals chosen for these CBI committees will normally, as in the case of Mike Flux, be executives of companies with a special interest in the regulation that the committees will deal with. It is in this way that individual firms are assured of representation in the regulation-making process.

While consultation is often continuous and is always available in the regulation-making process, the <u>HSE Guide to Regulation Making</u> outlines specific consultative steps to be used. In addition to the "formal consultation stage," which includes circulation of the Consultative Document, the <u>HSE Guide</u> requires extensive preliminary consultation, often referred to in other terms. For example:

<u>Exploratory contacts.</u> Industry and other outside bodies. CBI and TUC should be informed when there are written pro-

posals on major or significant topics for discussion with industry or outside bodies.

<u>Discussion of proposals.</u> Inform CBI, TUC, and local authority members of arrangements for initial circulation of any discussion papers involving their own members.

There are, in fact, six discrete points at which staff members are required to consider informal or preliminary consultation.

Consultative procedures thus involve two stages: formal consultation (characterized by the publication of draft regulations, called "Consultative Documents," which is analogous to publication in the United States of draft regulations in the Federal Register, followed by a period for public comment); and a much more complex informal stage which precedes the publication of the draft regulations.

The latter stage has no counterpart in the United States. It is in fact by all measures the most important of the two parts of the consultative processes, for informal consultation provides a forum for give and take between environmental interests — one that allows for the fine tuning of competing claims in the regulatory process, at a time when the regulations themselves are still in a formative state. This is the stage at which the "hard-nosed" negotiation, referred to by ICI's Mike Flux, takes place, with the result that when draft regulations are published, business as well as most public groups have been exposed to the contents and have argued for their interest in the regulation. This exposure, coupled with the tolerance bred of years of participation in the system, accounts for much of the relative ease with which the British adapt to new regulations. There is a feeling that new regulations represent a "consensus position" of the parties involved in regulatory outcomes.

There are several ways in which business benefits from the consultative process in Britain. While there is no evidence to suggest that businesspeople dominate the environmental policy process or, for that matter, unfairly (by British standards) influence regulations or their administration, business definitely participates in both technical and policy capacities. Certainly, self-interest is involved. It is the responsibility of government officials to see that interest is restrained for the benefit of the public. As Mike Flux pointed out, those officials always have the final say.

The primary benefit to business lies in its ability, through consultation, to make its ideas felt at early stages. This is equally true in regulation making and in the application of regulations to the operations of business. When regulations are made, consultation allows managers to make their views explicit and thus be satisfied that they have influenced the process to the best of their ability. Having done so, they are more willing to accept the resulting regulations without protest than are their American counterparts.

When business must adhere to established regulations, the opportunity to consult with regional government personnel, often to work out solutions to problems with the cooperation of these same people, provides cost savings and smoother operations. For example, when firms establish a new plant in Britain, it is customary to consult with regulatory authorities while plans are in the outline stage, and thus changes, if required, can be made at the least possible cost. Several potential sites may be considered, with the Department of the Environment or the HSE cooperating in the final selection process. Here, operating costs are considered side by side with environmental problems, and cost effectiveness for the country as a whole is invoked as an important criterion.

Consultation, then, is an important process underlying all British environmental regulation. It represents a principle of participation that is both democratic and practical. While both formal and informal consultation operate in the system, the informal aspect is, in fact, by far the most powerful. Though I have stressed the role of business in consultation, the process includes other important environmental stakeholders as well.

Informal consultation (as I defined it for the British case) holds enormous potential for use in the United States. Surely, here is a way to defuse much of the hostility inherent in the adversarial relationship we have discussed. With its potential for the exchange of ideas at flexible stages of regulation making and with its tendency to engage participants in the policy process and win their support for ensuing compromises, it is worthy of serious consideration in the design of any consultative system we may propose.

One aspect of informal or "early" consultation deserves added consideration here. Regulation making bears a strong resemblance to the policy formulation process in most large organizations. Both are characterized by a kind of hierarchy of decision making, which in general starts with preliminary staff work to gather data, followed by a review by management, and then by exhaustive staff work to recommend details of the policy or regulation. This work is then reviewed by individual managers before submission to a board, or committee of managers, for final evaluation and either modification or adoption. Often there are many iterations of one or more of these stages.

If this entire process is completed prior to submission to outsiders for comment (that is, via the British Consultative Document, or the U.S. Federal Register publication), experience shows that changes, no matter how appropriate, will be resisted, simply because positions have been taken during the policy process from which it is difficult to retreat. The internal process of persuasive give and take forces individuals to espouse solutions in such a way that it is hard to give them up without losing credibility in the organization. Thus, individuals come to identify with, and to have a personal stake in, specific policy elements or specific regulatory terms. In truth, the formal consultative stage in both countries is recognized more as a form that must be observed than as an opportunity to improve on policies being formulated.

Informal, "early" consultation, on the other hand, makes its contribution in the formative, flexible stages of policy development. Staff members are thus exposed to outside opinion and data _before_ they have need to harden their positions about the details of policy or regulations. Therefore, it is far more likely that legitimate positions of environmental stakeholders will be included in resultant regulations if inputs to the regulation-making process can be made in this timely way.

This chapter has provided a comparison of British and U.S. environmental regulation. We have concluded that the most important difference in these two systems lies in the British use of informal consultation to guide regulation makers and to allow industry and other stakeholders to express their views at early stages of the regulation process. The British also employ similar informal processes at the point of application of regulations. Both of these consultative elements hold promise for inclusion into U.S. policy. The chapters that follow will examine some specifics of how they can be applied to this country.

APPENDIX 7.1

Members of Advisory Committee on Toxic Substances

Miss L. A. Pittom (Chairwoman)
    Director of Hazardous Substances Division, Health and Safety
    Executive
Mr. R. N. Bottini
    General Secretary, National Union of Agricultural and Allied
    Workers
Dr. T. A. Connors
    Director, Medical Research Council Toxicology Unit
Dr. G. M. Davies
    Occupational Hygiene Unit, Research Centre, British Steel
    Corporation
Mr. F. Dyson
    General Secretary, National Union of Dyers, Bleachers and
    Textile Workers
Mr. J. F. Eccles
    National Officer, National Union of General and Municipal
    Workers
Mr. D. J. Barnett
    Chief Environmental Health Officer, Bristol District Council
Mr. J. P. Hamilton
    Social Insurance and Industrial Welfare Department, Trade
    Union Congress
Councillor R. M. Knowles
    West Midlands County Council
Dr. I. Laing
    Production Director, Clayton Aniline Co. Ltd.
Mr. D. A. Morgan
    General Manager and Chief Executive, Commonwealth Smelting
    Ltd.
Professor R. S. F. Schilling
    Former Professor of Occupational Health, London School of
    Hygiene and Tropical Medicine
Dr. M. Sharratt
    Environmental Health Unit, Research Centre, British Petroleum
    Co. Ltd.
Mr. D. G. Travis
    Personnel Director, Reed Building Products Ltd.
Dr. K. S. Williamson
    Principal Medical Officer, ICI Ltd.
Mr. A. W. Durham (Secretary)
    Toxics and Corrosive Branch, Health and Safety Executive

NOTES

1. The companies were the British Petroleum Company Ltd.,
Imperial Chemical Industries, Ltd., Rio Tinto Zinc Corporation,
British Gas Corporation, and Powell Duffryn Oil and Chemical
Storage Ltd. The British government agencies were the Health
and Safety Executive and the Thames Water Authority. Environmental organizations were the Environmental Data Service,
Friends of the Earth, and Public Interest Research Center Ltd.
2. Administration of British environmental regulation is
uniform throughout Britain, except in Scotland, which is a
special case. All Scottish law is handled by a single ministry,
the Scottish Department, to provide a measure of local autonomy.
Scottish environmental regulation closely follows the format
extant in the rest of Britain but is administered through subde-
partments of the Scottish Department. Interviews were not
conducted in Scotland.
3. For a more detailed description of this process, see Roy
Gregory, The Price of Amenity (London: Macmillan, 1971).
4. Quoted in Maurice Frankel, The Social Audit Pollution
Handbook (London: Macmillan, 1978), p. 64.
5. Draft regulations, entitled "Consultative Documents," are
published by British government agencies to allow the public a
six-month period to submit written comments on proposed regulations. They are the counterpart of publication by U.S. agencies
in the Federal Register for the same purpose.

8
Alternatives to Command-and-Control Regulation

So far in this book we have concentrated largely on an examination of the problems inherent in our present difficult system of environmental control. The reader may ask, with good reason, "what can be done about all of this?" I have made it clear that I favor consultative approaches to better regulation, but just how those might work out is certainly not readily apparent. It is clear that many people in government, industry, and the academic world have thought about how the regulatory process can be improved. I have tried to point out in Chapter 6 that there is an interest within the Reagan administration in improving the process, as well as making it "smaller." Economists have long advocated a variety of schemes revolving around the "pricing" of pollution, and though these have been rejected by Congress, other countries have experimented with them, with some success. It is also obvious that recently in both the Carter and Reagan administrations some very valuable progress has been made in the "offset trading" of pollution, resulting in the EPA's "bubble" and emission offset policies. In addition, in the past few years, the process of mediation, which has a long history in the labor and international relations fields, has provided an excellent consultative base for the settlement of selected environmental disputes.

Among these approaches there has been some valuable movement in the direction of consultation on environmental issues. They can point the way to additional progress in ways that are worthy of our attention.

PRICING POLLUTION

Economists tend to prefer an approach to pollution regulation that lets the market, subject to government standards, decide how much control is to be imposed at what sources. One reason market factors are in favor is that market systems can provide a direct linkage between costs and benefits that the producer and consumer can see and by which rational regulatory decisions can be made. Command-and-control systems filter the costs of regulation through government budgets and product-pricing systems in such a way that costs are obscured. When consumers receive the benefits of a cleaner environment without perceiving the costs, an infinite demand for more cleanliness is created, and many economists view this as a potentially serious distortion of the market system.

When pollution is priced (another way of saying that a charge is made for each increment of pollution), those who create pollution can choose whether to pay the charge and continue polluting or devise some way to stop or reduce pollution and proportionately reduce the charge. It should be evident that charges, if they are significant, must be passed on to consumers, and hence there will be competitive pressures to reduce the charges, and the pollution. The reduction of pollution thus takes on a very personal institutional character, which is in itself a stimulus for innovation and invention to internalize pollution costs. This incentive to innovate is largely absent from the operation of command-and-control systems, since the regulatory agency specifies, in general terms, the "best available technology" and the acceptable level of discharge. The only incentive is for producers to avoid the penalties of not reaching this level.

Both France and West Germany have experimented with pollution pricing, each with moderate success and the exposition of some problems. The West German experience is best seen in the use of the national water quality law of 1957 by the Ruhr Valley Water Associations.[1] The permit system of that legislation was designed to provide for the internalization of pollution externalities on a case-by-case basis. Charges were to be set proportional to the level of pollution of each individual producer, and permits to discharge would be issued in return for payment of the appropriate charge — a pollution-pricing system. Though the system has worked well in many instances, one serious problem has been the independence of the many water associations through which permits are issued. This has fostered variability in standards, which are often quite low (small reductions in pollution) and susceptible to local political influence.

While, in general, the 1957 law has resulted in an important improvement in the quality of Ruhr water, the system that has evolved has more of the earmarks of local law than of national legislation. It would not qualify as the sort of nationally coordinated and enforced control system envisioned by the U.S. Congress. Further, the charges used in the system are not based directly on the pollution produced, but surrogates such as product output or number of employees have been used in pricing the permits. These concessions to local political factors, on the one hand, and administrative costs, on the other, depart a long way from the economist's ideal of requiring producers to internalize all of their pollution costs, but nothing more.

The French water pollution experience has a more national scope than that of West Germany. The government began its first six-year plan in 1971, with moderately good results worked out through an efficient national administration, which has been praised throughout Europe. The plan is administered through a group of river-basin agencies, such as the Seine-Normandie Basin Association, which sets standards for their drainage areas. However, permits to discharge are actually issued by the local prefect rather than the basin agency. Discharge improvements are specified in each permit. A small pollution tax is levied by the basin agency, with the proceeds making up a pool that can be issued as grants to firms or communities for pollution control investment. Here, as in West Germany, the stated philosophy of the law is to require discharges to internalize their pollution costs through the application of charges and incentives to improve — again, a pollution-pricing system. The French, however, seem to have been as skillful as the West Germans at avoiding the actual practice of attaching a price to a kilogram of pollution. Instead, the use of scheduled improvements to qualify for permits is the preferred incentive device. While there may be an incentive to reduce pollution and to innovate, the effect of obscuring costs so disliked by economists is just as much present in the French system as it is in the U.S. command-and-control format.

A recent U.S. EPA study hypothetically planned a pollution-pricing system for Chicago and identified the costs that might be associated with such a program. The conclusions were enlightening. The study attempted to cost-out several alternate methods of controlling emissions of nitrogen dioxide. While no national short-term standards have yet been set for this contaminant, it is thought to have significant health effects and will probably figure in future EPA regulations.[2] The study considered the effects and costs associated with 146 plants that produce the preponderance of this pollutant in the Chicago area. It further specified a short-term standard of 250 micrograms per cubic meter of air. Present command-and-control methods were calculated to cost $130 million per year. The staff then calculated the costs of imposing a uniform emissions charge of

$15,800 per pound of nitrogen dioxide per hour per year. This would be the pollution price. The total costs were staggering: $715 million a year. These were made up of $414 million for emissions charges and $305 million for control equipment. The explanation for the very high cost of this approach is that operations in a few locations in Chicago, such as coal-fired boilers, were very expensive to clean up. To provide an incentive for these operations to improve, EPA had set the price per pound of pollution at a very high level. Under this pricing system, other polluters would have an incentive to clean up far more than necessary to meet the standard of 250 micrograms.

The system that economists would readily like to see is one that would provide each plant with about the same incentive, regardless of how difficult the cleanup job. This would require a different price per pound for pollution, depending on the type of operation a producer was conducting. Assuming that there was a great deal of uniqueness, EPA calculated the costs of cleanup incentives on a plant-by-plant basis — theoretically the best way. On this basis, the costs would drop to an eye-opening $13 million, just 10 percent of the cost of command-and-control. But there is a catch, and it is a big one. The administrative costs of operating such a customized program, with all of the independent testing, modeling, and pricing based on specific plant characteristics would be so high and the red tape so cumbersome that the savings of the approach would probably be eaten up in the process.

Most economists hold that the greatest benefit of pollution pricing is to encourage industry to look at pollution as an economic problem and then to bring its usual economic decision processes to bear on that problem. The costs of pollution can then be seen in the same light as any other production cost. Businesses will accordingly bring all of their cost consciousness to bear on the problems of reducing pollution through investment, innovation, product design, and other relevant variables.

From the viewpoint of regulators, however, and this includes the European staffs as well as the EPA, the costs of setting pollution prices and administering a workable system with the elegant detail required to make it effective is just too high.

One result of our experience with pollution pricing to date has been a lingering refrain in the minds of economists, businesspeople, and regulators that the pricing ideal would be fine, if only it could be administered on a practical basis.

OFFSET TRADING

One way to get a limited number of the benefits of pollution pricing with much less administrative cost is to allow a plant to reduce the most flagrant emission processes, or the cheapest to control, within the plant complex and to measure the <u>total</u> output of pollutants instead of regulating every machine that creates a problem. In this way, a company can concentrate its efforts on the conspicuous offenders among its processes. If it reduces some emissions below the requirements, it may continue to pollute with other processes that would perhaps be more expensive to control.

This approach has, in fact, been pioneered by the EPA and is known as the "bubble." The idea is that a manufacturer can put all of its processes at any one location under a theoretical "bubble," trading emissions at one process for reductions at another, so long as the total pollution from the bubble does not exceed permissible limits. To a large extent, the bubble does provide incentive to innovate, and it introduces economic thinking into the pollution decision process to the extent that a producer can figure out the cheapest way to achieve acceptable emissions for the <u>specific</u> operations involved.

When this concept is extended to an entire community, it is known as "offset trading" or controlled trading." Under this broader concept, if a manufacturer wishes to build a plant that is expensive to control, the manufacturer may, with permission from EPA, contribute to a reduction in emissions of another plant within the same pollution control district, thus balancing the total emissions for the area. This often takes the form of agreement to make a financial contribution to the pollution control equipment of another manufacturer.

One of the reasons why offset trading is so attractive is the enormous variation in control costs between industries. The average cost to remove pollutants in high control-cost industries, say nonferrous metals, is about 100 times that in low control-cost industries, such as some chemicals. Such programs augur well for cost savings, as well as innovation.

For example, under the bubble concept, the 3M Company will save $5 million at its Bristol, Pennsylvania, plant this year by substituting water-based coatings and a new solventless hot-melt process to substantially reduce emissions on three production lines, in return for easier controls on seven other lines.[3]

As an example of offset trading, the management at General Portland Cement paid Parker Brothers $520,000 to install dust collectors at its New Braunfels, Texas, plant. In return, EPA has allowed General Portland to install a coal-fired preheater at its plant in the same community. The combination of these two moves will still keep the area within the EPA health standards for particulates and will result in substantial savings for the cement company.[4]

EPA has recently experimented with a concept to extend offset trading, an admittedly limited kind of activity, through a system of "banking." The concept here is that if a firm voluntarily reduces its emissions below requirements, say by substituting natural gas for coal as a fuel, it may sell a kind of "permit to pollute" to a bank, which in turn will complete the swap at some later time to another producer wishing to install equipment emitting more than EPA allows. Such "banks" would be specialized entities, set up for the purpose of effecting the delicate exchanges required in offset trading. The cumbersome and technical process of brokering these "licenses" has not attracted a great deal of interest. I personally do not foresee a great future in such a market mechanism.

MEDIATION

While judicial confrontation between environmental stakeholders continues to be the norm of behavior in policy disagreements, there are signs that both industry and environmental groups are becoming aware of the possible benefits of mediation. This technique, born largely of the need for extrajudicial settlements of labor relations disputes, also has roots in international negotiation.

Interest in the process has spawned several private, nonprofit mediation services around the country during the last few years. Of these, the most prominent is probably the Institute for Environmental Mediation (IEM) in Seattle. Mediators are normally jointly paid by the parties to a dispute, and they act as facilitators in the negotiation of a settlement, if one is possible. Such a settlement must constitute a consensus of views of all the parties. Settlements are reduced to binding agreements between the parties but do not require review by the courts.

As an example of the kind of work that mediators do, and of the implications for consultation, let us review a case that was successfully mediated recently by IEM.[5]

When the mediators entered the Pitch Mine dispute, Homestake Mining Company and several Colorado conservation groups had been arguing for four years over what constituted adequate land restoration after the strip mining of uranium at the company's Pitch Mine site in Colorado's Gunnison National Forest.

The firm had complied with the legal requirements for commencement of mining operations. An Environmental Impact Statement (EIS) had been prepared by the U.S. Forest Service and, based on this and additional technical data, permits had been issued by the Colorado Department of Natural Resources, Division of Mined Land Reclamation, and the Colorado Department of Health, Division of Water Quality Control.

Still, there were special circumstances in this case, and the conservation groups formed a coalition to oppose the mining operations. Included in the coalition were the Colorado Wildlife Federation, Colorado Open Space Council, Gunnison Valley Alliance, Gold Hill Committee on Mining and the Environment, and High Country Citizens Alliance. The coalition, which retained the Natural Resources Law Clinic in Boulder, Colorado, to represent them, claimed that special circumstances in the case had rendered the EIS inadequate. These included the facts that the mine was to be situated above 10,000 feet in altitude with possible problems of revegetation; the steep slopes posed difficult erosion and wildlife management problems; and water, health, and safety issues were involved.

This will sound like a familiar litany to many managers. In fact, Homestead, though vowing it had a very good case, took the coalition's complaints seriously enough to be willing to enter mediation with them. The company felt that, in the words of its attorney, John L. Watson, "court action would be too costly in time and money."6

Among the key issues that formed the first stage of the mediator's agenda was a set of closely defined, specific limits for the issues to be discussed. This spelled out not only what would be included in the mediation process, but what would **not** be included as well. At this stage, the parties also agreed not to include government agencies in the process, but instead to keep the agencies informed of relevant developments. They further agreed to keep their discussions private. Comments to the press were limited to procedural matters.

The complexity of the many overlays of issues faced by the negotiators was daunting. In addition to issues of substance, the communications problem was to prove substantial. Not only did the Homestake management require regular corporate briefings, but the coalition, with its many members and affiliations, needed to keep all of its constituents informed of progress and to take advice from those interested parties. The mediators were required to use an "issues flow chart" to keep track of the many facets of negotiation and decisions agreed upon.

The mediation process in this dispute consumed just under a year of time. Its result was an agreement in three parts. First, a <u>Statement of Understanding</u> agrees on the measures to be used as the mining proceeds. Second, a <u>Mediation Agreement</u> commits Homestake to an ongoing relationship with the coalition to provide information and sponsor reclamation research. Third, a <u>Covenant Not to Sue</u> signed by each of the coalition members provides Homestake with good assurance that it can proceed without harrassment.

The outcomes of the mediation process were presented to the public in a joint press release, which stated the reasons of the parties for their commitment and underlined the fact that basic conflicts in values persisted that would continue to characterize their organizations.

The mediation process, as it was used at Pitch Mine, is an excellent example of consultation at work in the environmental arena. The especially complex task of bringing together a wide spectrum of interests to obtain consensus on ways to protect the environment while proceeding with an inherently polluting mining operation suggests a variety of techniques for the application of consultation to U.S. environmental problems.

POLICY DIALOGUES

There have been several encouraging attempts in the last few years to bridge the gap between environmental stakeholders for the purpose of defining areas of mutual agreement on issues. These represent the coming together of fairly diverse interests, with the participants really intent on bettering their individual positions by the extrajudicial processes of negotiation and consultation. In each case, participants have reported a growth in trust and cooperation as a result of the bargaining process. The outcomes for interest groups have been at least as good as was expected of the judicial process, always at much lower cost, and this has been true for <u>each side</u> in the discussions. Let us examine four of these processes here.

The Health Effects Institute

The Health Effects Institute was founded by the EPA in December 1980, during the Carter administration, and has been reinforced by the Reagan administration. It is funded by a grant from Congress and contributions from U.S. auto manufacturers, as well as by more than a dozen auto-importing companies. Its responsibility is to generate and evaluate health data about automobile emissions.

The institute is headed by a three-member board of directors including Archibald Cox, professor at Harvard Law School, Donald Kennedy, president at Stanford University, and William O. Baker, chairman of Rockefeller University. It has been described by Cox as "fiercely independent."[7]

The mission to generate health data is expected to ease several long-standing problems between EPA and the auto industry. These include duplication and inefficiency in gathering data, lack of consistency and compatability between the industry and EPA in research methods, and the ineffective use of scarce research facilities.

The directors appoint two scientific boards, who in turn establish policy and oversee results and publication of scientific data. These are the Health Research Board and the Health Review Board. Both are staffed with eminent scientists from the diverse fields needed to carry out the institute's mission. The Health Effects Institute is laying the groundwork for a nonpartisan, trustworthy approach to protecting the public health without the adversarial mistrust presently inherent in the roles of the industry and government participants in the auto emissions regulatory process. The most encouraging aspect of the program is the voluntary participation by adversaries in a cooperative scientific process.[8]

The National Coal Policy Project

The National Coal Policy Project was formed to address the complex environmental problems associated with the mining and burning of coal. It consists of representatives from leading environmental groups and the coal industry. The EPA, while interested in the proceedings, has not joined in the formal procedures of the project. The group came into being because participants were dissatisfied with the extended judicial and regulatory battles they had experienced.

Their working methods are to inspect field sites where there has been dissatisfaction with the regulatory process and to gather and process data. In this stage of their work, project members have been accompanied by representatives of Georgetown University as an independent third party. From this data the group has worked out rules and standards to satisfy both environmentalists and industry members. The process has resulted in the execution of more than 200 agreements between the parties. Based on their investigative and consultative work, the group has presented several proposed amendments of the Clean Air Act to Congress. The project is supported financially by foundation grants and contributions from the coal industry.

The Tripartite Committee

During 1980 the Tripartite Committee, composed of EPA officials, representatives of the U.S. steel industry, and members of the United Steelworkers Union, convened to hammer out an agreement for a legislative amendment to be proposed to Congress to help the industry modernize, control pollution in the inherently dirty steelmaking business, and protect the jobs of workers in the process. The three groups, which have traditionally been hostile to each other, found the meetings difficult at first. There seemed to be no common ground — no equitable solutions to the industry's problems that all three could approve of.

Gradually, over a period of months of frustrating speech-making and posturing on all sides, solutions began to gel. Partly because the group had set a deadline, it was forced to examine the realities of the industry, each from the other's point of view. A form of agreement slowly emerged, which eventually resulted in the proposal that had been sought. In the words of Michele Corash, EPA general counsel and one of the participants:

> It wasn't at all easy. I think that every single person in the process was accused by his colleagues and by those back home of selling out. But in the end we got a product that we were all fairly satisfied with, and that to a large degree accomplished our goals. We all had to give up something, but we all got more than we probably would have gotten any other way.[9]

U.S. Steel Corporation's Cooperative Assessment

When U.S. Steel began planning for its proposed new $4 billion Lakefront Steel Mill at Conneaut, Ohio, recently, managers considered the possibility of trying to avoid the usual adversarial hassle with government agencies, the community, and the courts by using a cooperative approach. In the past the company had experienced delays of several years in getting approval of its Environmental Impact Statements and construction permits. What managers hoped for this time was quicker approval and wider acceptance by environmentalists and the local community, through a process of disseminating information and listening to input from others. It was decided to attempt an assessment process prior to the submission of EIS data to the Army Corps of Engineers, the lead agency for the project. The firm's managers were assisted by their consultant, Arthur D. Little, Inc.

The process that they chose was built around two coordinating committees, one executive and the other technical. Each group included managers from U.S. Steel, representatives from several levels of government, and members of community organizations. The executive group was responsible for forming and directing meetings, seminars, and other information exchange media to enable groups and individuals to learn about the project and to express their concerns. It also took responsibility for directing the assessment procedure to assure that the project conformed to all applicable environmental statutes and regulations.

The technical group was responsible for the accuracy of technical data and an unbiased evaluation of scientific materials. It is worth noting that one of the danger areas for discussions of this kind is the varying interpretation of scientific data by different groups, hence the importance to the project of a cooperative technical approach.

The results of the cooperative assessment appear to be favorable. The draft EIS was prepared in a period of 16 months. It is normal for this process to require three to four years. Furthermore, an assessment of the climate of cooperation among the participants and the outlook for avoiding future conflict suggests that the procedure was successful in building a favorable climate for the completion of the mill.[10]

In summary, while I will have to admit that there is a great deal of appeal to the economist's preference for a pollution-pricing system that would make environmental regulation subject to market factors, and hence relatively self-policing within the enterprise system, I do not see pollution pricing as a viable policy. The program costs would seem to be much too high, and the administrative complexity threatens to defeat the elegant simplicity of the economic formulation.

I have a lot of respect for the people at EPA who are working to implement offset trading even further than it has progressed to date. This work can achieve a substantial part of the goal to spur innovation and make managers individually conscious of the need to design pollution control into their operations. There is a good chance that this work will be expanded, as well it should.

Our most important need now is to ease the difficult adversarial relationship that exists between all of the stakeholders in the environmental arena. If this can be done, offset trading, fairer regulations, and indeed many other benefits will begin to flow for the interests of all citizens. We have seen some of these benefits unfold in the examples of mediation and policy dialogues discussed above. These can be the true forerunners of a consultative policy to protect the environment and at the same time advance economic and human well-being that is so often neglected under command-and-control regulation. In the following chapter, I will try to explain how I think this can be accomplished.

NOTES

1. R. W. Johnson and G. M. Brown, Cleaning Up Europe's Waters (New York: Praeger, 1976), p. 128.

2. Tom Alexander, "A Simpler Path to a Cleaner Environment," Fortune, May 4, 1981, p. 253.

3. William Drayton, "Thinking Ahead: Getting Smarter About Regulation," Harvard Business Review 59 (July-August 1981), pp. 38-52.

4. Ibid.

5. Orville M. Tice, "The Pitch Mine Case," Institute for Environmental Mediation, Seattle, 1981.

6. "Environment," Business Week, January 18, 1982.

7. Quoted in J. Ronald Fox, "Breaking the Regulatory Deadlock," Harvard Business Review 59 (September-October 1981), pp. 97-105.

8. Ibid., p. 101.

9. Michele B. Corash, quoted in Corporations and the Environment: How Should Decisions Be Made?, Graduate School of Business, Stanford University, 1981, pp. 73-74.

10. R. D. Ortina and S. B. Lundstedt, "Cooperative Assessment Procedures under the National Environmental Policy Act," Toxic Substances Journal (Fall 1980), pp. 150-160. Since the assessment program, a change in U.S. Steel's policy has required the indefinite postponement of the Lakefront mill.

9
A Proposal for Change

A few years ago, a colleague, who does a great deal of industrial consulting, was called upon by a major steel company to evaluate the state of pollution control at one of its mills. The firm's managers wanted to know, as closely as possible, what it would cost to bring the entire mill operation into compliance with federal regulations. Included in the consultant's task was the recommendation of new, state-of-the-art production equipment, where it would facilitate pollution control and was reasonably economic.

This was a large, dirty mill that operated under difficult atmospheric conditions and had plagued the community with noxious air pollution for years. The company had been cited repeatedly by the EPA for noncompliance with regulations. It had won several reprieves in the courts to enable it to study and obtain the "best available technology" to resolve the pollution problems on the site. The firm had, over the years, installed considerable stopgap equipment to reduce harmful emissions, but this was never enough to overcome the pollution problems of the basic mill equipment. Installed during and shortly after World War II, it was inherently dirty. One of the corporate directors, a key operating manager, confided to my colleague, "We are tired of fighting legal battles, with their attendant costs. We are in the steel business, not the litigation business — all of this sparring takes time, costs a great deal of money, and detracts from our managing of the stockholders' interests."

My friend began the assignment optimistically by reviewing the EPA regulations and relating them to the various production operations. He consulted with managers in the firm, with lawyers who specialize in the field, and with suppliers of pollution control and basic steelmaking equipment. The more he studied the problem, the more troubled he became. This was not going to be an economic study, as he had anticipated, but an exercise in moral judgment!

The consultant's calculations demonstrated quite conclusively that the best way for the firm to earn an acceptable return on its stockholders' investment was for managers to <u>pretend</u> that they intended to reduce pollution to acceptable levels, while continuing to produce with the present equipment. The costs of going to court, attempting to obtain delays in enforcement, paying fines, and installing limited pollution control equipment for the cosmetic purpose of deceiving the public would have been so much less than the costs of solving the problems that there was truly no economic basis for comparison of the two.

To have stated that they did not intend to cure the problem would have invited a court order to shut down the mill. To invest the staggering sums calculated to bring operations into compliance would not only have been uneconomic; it was improbable that the firm could find the money to do the job. What was really needed was replacement of almost the entire complement of the mill's production equipment. The company's capital structure just would not support the additional investment. Yet, <u>functionally</u> the operations had many years of economic steel-making left.

What had turned out to be the most economically feasible solution was not, based on my colleague's extensive interviews, what the management desired at all. Nor had they anticipated that the study would point in this direction. This was simply the first time that all of the firm's options had been considered "in the same shop."

The consultant, being a reputable businessman, was loath to advise a strategy that involved lying to the public, with the further implications of perjury in the courts. There were few satisfactions in the assignment. His dilemma was, however, less palpable than that of his client. In the end, he presented a report that delineated the costs of two alternate behaviors: revitalizing the mill to meet the existing regulations, but at tremendous cost; and a "skating along" strategy, infinitely more desirable economically, but involving deception and a degree of moral turpitude that was both undesirable and unlikely of conspiracy among the firm's managers. He made no recommendation for action.

It seems to me that, among the many curious ingredients in this dilemma, the most insidious are elements of the laws and attendant regulations designed to protect the environment. If readers will accept that it would have been desirable for society to protect the quality of the local air, the jobs of the mill workers, and the investment of the company's stockholders, all in some measure at the same time, then they should agree that some form of compromise would have been highly desirable. The fact was, for all of the reasons discussed in the previous chapters, compromise was legally and tactically impossible. The company was forced into an excruciating dichotomy of undesirable solutions, neither of which would have served the mutual interests of the stakeholders mentioned.

It may seem to some readers that a form of social Darwinism is operating here — that the fittest must survive, and many investments and jobs will inevitably be wiped out in the cause of a clean environment. To shrug off public responsibility for the casualties of regulation is indeed somewhat fashionable, yet it is not inevitable that we live through procrustean solutions to every problem of public policy. The public knows how to cooperate by meshing the interests of the community with that of business to gain compromise victories over conflict. Consider the well-publicized problems of the Chrysler Corporation.

The monumental turnaround at Chrysler would not have been even vaguely possible without the cooperation, against tremendous odds, of Congress, the United Autoworkers and its membership, Chrysler, and a syndicate of commercial banks. Hovering on the very edge of failure in 1980, with a loss of $1.7 billion for the year, it seemed the company and 350,000 jobs dependent on Chrysler would disappear before our eyes. Under the pressure of this crisis, with the leadership of Lee A. Iacocca, the stakeholders in Chrysler's future put together a compromise that was to save the company, bail out the banks that loaned it money, and sustain the jobs of most Chrysler workers and probably 200,000 others indirectly dependent on the existence of the firm.

The rush of events that made the rescue possible will be under study at business schools for a generation. Certainly the agreement of Congress to a $1.5 billion loan guarantee to enable Chrysler to borrow at the banks long enough to put a new competitive strategy into place was vital. The strategy itself was masterful and suited to the situation. But key to the loan guarantee, and the train of events that followed, was the spirit of compromise and mutual interest that was forged between the interested parties.

Each of the direct parties grudgingly gave up something it considered important in the interest of Chrysler's survival. Banks rescheduled debt, accepting equity in place of some short-term assets. Union members accepted reduced compensation and fringe benefits. The company slashed management structures, eliminating whole layers and departments of managers and white-collar workers in the interests of efficiency. It agreed to the presence of a union representative on its board of directors (totally without precedent in U.S. industry). Chrysler's employment dropped from 130,000 in 1979 to 74,000 in 1982, and much of the drop was through elimination of white-collar jobs.

The result has been a reduction of the company's break-even point by half, to 1.2 million vehicles per year, an increase in market share from 7 to 10 percent, and a profit increase from a $1.7 billion loss in 1980 to an expected gain of $900 million in 1983. As this book is being written, the firm has announced that it has achieved a $1.5 billion cash surplus from which it has just repaid the last $800 million of government guaranteed loans — seven years ahead of schedule.

Observers agree that equally as important as the funds made available by federal loan guarantees was the spirit of cooperation between stakeholders that evolved under pressure from Congress. In the words of Martin Anderson, professor at MIT, "The loan guarantee was stated in terms of matching, so everyone had to come to a common table. They fought a lot, but eventually they had to cooperate and that forced a common constituency."[1]

While our rigid laws and nonconsultative procedures certainly prohibit a solution like that of Chrysler to any major environmental problem at the present time, the spirit of mutual purpose displayed in that incident has too often been present in the solution of environmental dilemmas in other countries for us to dismiss the likelihood of such negotiation in the United States. What Congress has done, it can modify or undo if it makes sense to do so. It surely makes sense to revise our environmental laws to allow for consultation at several stages. Let us look at just how this might be done.

To begin with, the range of problems that consultation can benefit is enormous. When I raise the possibility of consultation with managers, I find them enthusiastic about applying it to the legislative process, to the formulation of regulations, and to the implementation of regulations at every level of operations. In the words of the environmental control manager of a midwestern metal-fabricating plant:

> What we need is a sense of priorities. Some pollution problems can be solved here with quick fixes. Others require a long-range capital budgeting and equipment replacement program. The way we operate now is to put out the fire when we have to and hope that we are not caught on a process which needs a really expensive fix. If we could lay our cards on the table with EPA and work out some long-range programs, it would cost us less, and we would be a cleaner plant immediately.

According to the president of a Florida nitrate producer:

> If we could consult with EPA in a really meaningful way, I am sure we could suggest modifications in the

regulations affecting our industry which would improve our pollution performance without costing the industry much at all. As it is, we seem to fight with them every time we have contact.

In searching for a place to begin the consultative process, I have found it useful to ask myself some questions about the future of consultation in the United States. Three that will best transmit the meaning of my inquiry are the following: What types of problems are conducive to consultation? Who should participate in consultation? What structure and processes will succeed in bringing about consultative solutions in the United States? Each of these is worthy of some rather careful thought. They are listed with supporting detail in Table 9.1.

WHAT TYPES OF PROBLEMS ARE CONDUCIVE TO CONSULTATION?

I believe that, in the right circumstances, consultation can benefit the regulation process in an almost infinite variety of ways. Consider the role of the British Royal Commission, which consults with diverse parties to the social scene, as it attempts to define the need for a new law. Recall also the role of British alkali inspectors, making the rounds of registered works, consulting with engineers and plant managers over the details of specific equipment, and considering how its functions can be improved to protect the environment. Japanese pollution inspectors at the prefecture or local level constantly consult as they apply the philosophy of "administrative guidance" but purposefully nudge business into compliance with the law.

While it is my fervent hope that we will someday see consultation at work in as wide a variety of situations as exist in Europe and Japan, I recognize, as I am sure the reader will, that this depth and diversity of cooperation cannot come about instantly in the United States. The hostility and deeply ingrained adversarial roles described in Chapter 5 will not be eliminated simply with the enactment of new legislation or the issuance of a presidential executive order. We will need to start the process of consultation as we would initiate any other social change — with leadership. We will need to focus the attention of all of the participants in environmental policy formulation and administration on the most critical areas, those that have the greatest meaning in terms of benefits and those that now cost the most.

It is imperative that we give the process of consultation a chance to work right at the top, in the formulation of regulations. The EPA and other environmental regulation agencies should have the opportunity to consult with industry and others

TABLE 9.1

The Proposed U.S. Environmental Consultation Service (ECS)

Types of Environmental Problems for Consultation	Participants in Consultation	Structure and Processes
A. Formulation of regulations. B. Major projects that affect the environment.	General rule: Involve all parties who have a vital interest. Specific parties, as appropriate: 1. Industry representatives, trade associations, etc., where entire industry is involved. 2. Specific developer, company, or government agency. 3. Regulation agency of jurisdiction. 4. Other interested federal agencies. 5. State and local unions. 6. Labor unions. 7. Technical experts from government, universities, and industry. 8. Environmental groups.	A. Basic elements: 1. Early consultation. 2. Include all parties with vital interests. 3. Regulating agency must make final decisions. 4. Consultative mechanisms must fit cultural norms and governmental practices. B. Environmental Consultation Service and procedures. 1. Regulating agencies submit draft regulations. 2. ECS decides on parties to consultation. 3. Set deadlines. 4. Establish subcommittees on technical or procedural matters. 5. Carry out mediating role. 6. Enforce limited confidentiality. 7. Publish report detailing outcomes of consultation.

who have legitimate interests in the regulatory process, on a face-to-face basis, in a forum where the details of proposed regulations can be subjected to the closest scrutiny.

In addition, there are major projects that affect a sufficiently wide range of environmental or economic interests that they should receive the substantial benefits that are obtainable only from wide-ranging and detailed consultation. Such projects include the Northern Tier Pipeline Company plan, which was described in the Introduction, and proposals of major environmental sensitivity, such as the expansion of national forest areas to include additional redwood lands in northern California. In issues of this magnitude, consultation cannot only offer the most distinguished service to the nation, but the example set by the process will provide the strongest form of leadership to encourage its use at lower levels of contact.

These two critical areas, regulation making and the planning of major projects, can serve as the proving ground for the specifics of consultation policy in the United States and in the process can point the way to a daily practice of cooperation between environmental stakeholders. There is no more effective way to remove the barriers of distrust between those interested in the environment than to involve them in cooperation in the formulation of policy of in the difficult bargaining that requires compromise and the surrender of some strongly held views in the achievement of mutually tenable solutions to a major environmental problem.

WHO SHOULD PARTICIPATE IN CONSULTATION?

Clearly, consultation must involve those parties who have vital interests in the regulation or the project that is being considered. This will include representatives of the industry or governmental units to be regulated or, in the case of a project, representatives of the firm or government agency proposing the project. Thus, regulations proposed to control chemical wastes should be discussed with representatives of the chemical industry as a whole. As we have seen, this is widely practiced in Europe, where trade associations are organized to take responsibility for this kind of activity.

Though trade associations in the United States do not serve this function except in rare instances, it is entirely feasible for industries to develop such a component. In fact, trade association officials with whom I have spoken have expressed a good deal of interest in advancing such groups.

In the case of major environmentally sensitive projects, such as the Northern Tier Pipeline, the firm or developing government agency itself should be represented. Whether other firms in the same industry, perhaps representing competing interests, should be included will depend on the specifics of the case. The aim should be to include all elements that are vitally interested.

The regulatory agency of jurisdiction should, of course, be included in the consultation group. In addition, it is possible that other federal agencies whose policies may be affected by the regulation or project under review would be an appropriate addition to the process. I have quoted Lester Lave who pointed out that the automobile exhaust provisions of the 1970 Clean Air Act seriously complicated the policy of another federal agency in reducing fuel consumption. For example, the participation of representatives of the Energy Department, in discussions leading to emission regulations for automobiles and some stationary sources, would lead to the examination of conflicting priorities of that type.

In some cases, regulations or projects will have a critical impact on local or state government, and hence members of those entities should be part of the consultation. Offshore oil drilling, hydroelectric projects, and major plant siting are examples of this sort of problem.

Labor unions may have a legitimate interest in representing their members in environmental consultation. The steel industry is one arena in which the introduction of pollution-reducing methods or machinery may affect either standing contracts or the general interests of union membership. The Tripartite Committee, discussed in Chapter 8, which represented the interests of the steel industry, the EPA, and the United Steelworkers Union, is an example of the need for union participation.

Technical expertise is frequently important to the understanding of consultative issues. The reader will have noted in Chapter 7 that the British consultation system includes technical specialists from universities, government, and industry to provide guidance in such matters. The U.S. Congress, in fact, utilizes specialists, often on an individual consultant basis, to support committee judgment. The employment of Lynton Caldwell as an expert in governmental process by the Senate Interior and Insular Affairs Committee during the development of NEPA is one of many powerful precedents for the utilization of such expertise.

A fundamental participant in the consultation process, in addition to all of the others, must be representatives of the environmental organizations described in Chapter 3, which have been so instrumental in the development of political awareness about environmental issues. For all of the reasons suggested in previous chapters, the environmental movement, represented by a handful of articulate, politically aware groups, has come to mean protection of the environment to a very substantial proportion of U.S. citizens. It is only fair that representatives of these groups be included. I am convinced that no structure for consultation could be approved by Congress unless it included participation by these private agencies. The inclusion of representatives of the environmental organizations will be critical to the outcomes of individual consultative issues.

It will also go a long way toward forging a community of interest about the environment, with beneficial effects on the adversarial relationship. Examples of consultation at work both here and in other countries point to this vitally important fact. The evidence of Chrysler Corporation and many other difficult situations provide dramatic testimony to the rewards of discussion between adversaries in the face of problems over which they have mutual concerns. The forging of consensus about the ways in which we need to protect the environment must be a vital part of the consultative process, and discussions must include all influential stakeholders.

WHAT STRUCTURE AND PROCESSES SHOULD BE USED?

Before discussing specific systems for the United States, we will briefly review the present role of consultation in Europe, Japan, and finally the United States.

The European systems preference (exemplified by the British systems outlined in Chapter 7) is for discussion of regulation through direct mechanisms in the regulating agency. Recall that the Health and Safety Executive in the British government maintains seven standing advisory groups with which it is required to consult where the experience of the group is appropriate. Beyond this, consultation is required with individuals and groups included on an extensive list of trade associations and other organizations called the "Formal Consultation List." An additional imperative of British, and other European, systems is that consultation is always confidential.

At the operating level, consultation takes place between regional inspectors and industry. The flexibility allowed these local civil servants provides the basis for specific practical negotiation over the form that regulations will take.

The Japanese prefer to make all regulations at the national level with limited consultation, but with a great deal of flexibility allowed to the local inspectors who apply the philosophy of "administrative guidance," often to the extent of establishing pollution limits right in the field. Thus, consultation at the "grass roots" level affects the application of national laws, providing for special circumstances and economic needs.

Some authorities argue that when Congress set up informal rule making within the federal Administrative Procedures Act it intended to prescribe a limited sort of consulting system. Informal rule making is the procedure under which the vast majority of environmental regulations are made. The procedure simply requires that proposed rules be published in the Federal Register and that after a suitable period of time in which to receive comments the agency may then enforce the regulation. As pointed out in Chapter 5, the courts have destroyed any consultative aspects attached to this procedure, by prohibiting the proposing agency from engaging in discussions with interested parties. Instead, the agency is left to rely wholly on written comments. It must be abundantly clear that, in the terms of reference used in this book, such one-sided communication is not consultation at all.

The history of consultation indicates that, to be successful, consultative mechanisms must include at least four basic elements.

1. Consultation must take place _early_ in the consideration of a policy or project.
2. Consultation must include all parties who have vital interests in the outcomes of the process.
3. The regulating agency must retain the right to make final decisions, after appropriate consultation. Consultation is not a substitute for agency staff work of agency decision making.
4. Consultative mechanisms must fit the cultural norms and governmental practices of the country in which they operate. No one country can simply copy practices that work in another.

Given these four principles and the general outline of the proceeding sections in this chapter, I envision a consultation structure somewhat like the following.

Consultation would take place under the auspices of a unique federal government agency, designed to bring together stakeholders in the environment, including the appropriate federal regulatory agency. For purposes of this discussion, I will call the agency the United States Environmental Consultation Service, or simply ECS.

Agencies responsible for environmental regulations would be required to submit draft regulations to the ECS for consideration and to participate in the consultative process of ECS. Officials of ECS would be responsible for deciding, within statutory requirements, who should participate in a given consultation. I have suggested participants early in this chapter, but that list is by no means exhaustive. The general principle of point 2 above should hold, namely that all who have a vital interest in the outcomes should be involved.

Specific consultation deadlines would be set for each draft regulation. These would be agreed by the parties to the process insofar as possible, with consideration given to the special character and technical nature of the subject.

Working parties or subcommittees would be assigned the task of recommending technical details and requirements. It is at this point that industry experts would have an opportunity to contribute to a realistic assessment of the technical parameters of the regulation.

The ECS would conduct sufficient meetings of the interested parties to provide a reasonable chance for consensus on the issues. While it may not always be possible for competing interests to agree, this should be the goal of the process. The role of ECS staff in the discussions should be a mediating one, aimed at producing outcomes that can be accepted by all of the parties. The process of mediation is well understood, with a well-defined body of literature. It should be utilized in the operation of ECS.[2]

The ECS would produce a summary report or "white paper" detailing the areas of agreement on the issues and stating the views of consultative parties on issues for which there is not agreement. The summary report should be given wide circulation and should be the basis for the final decisions made by the federal agency charged with making the regulation.

Consultation about a major project that would qualify for ECS services would proceed along much the same lines as outlined above. Projects would qualify if they fell within the guidelines suggested earlier in this chapter. Major projects should be submitted to ECS when they are in the outline stages. This can be defined as being as soon as sufficient technical and economic data is available for the participants to gain a clear understanding of the impacts of the project. Present law would require an Environmental Impact Statement for such a project, and an impact statement would be a natural starting place for consultation. Additional data might well be required to suit the mediation process.

It cannot be emphasized too strongly that the value of this kind of consulting process is at its greatest early in the history of a project or regulation — before views are hardened in concrete. While early review would be automatic in the case of regulations, every effort should be made to encourage protagonists in projects of an environmentally sensitive nature to qualify for ECS services as early as possible. It might be feasible, for example, to utilize an early notice process, in which firms or government agencies wishing to institute a project could submit outline data for several alternatives being considered and obtain guidance from other interested parties. This form of prior discussion, which is utilized by the British, is of enormous help in the planning stages of major projects. As in the case of consultation about regulations, ECS would be required to produce a report on the results of consultation. It would detail the areas of consensus among the parties, and the issues, if any, on which the participants could not agree. This report would provide developers with a strong probabilistic estimate of the chances for successful permitting. It would also be useful evidence in the permitting process.

It is natural that some will be concerned about the issue of confidentiality in consultations such as I am proposing. We have seen that the successful British and continental European consultative approaches involve a great deal of confidentiality. The consultative process involves negotiations, and negotiations are always best conducted away from the public eye. There are two powerful arguments in favor of confidentiality, and a very important principle opposing it.

First, an important consideration in any negotiation is that the public utterances of any of the parties may tend to polarize the stand of the negotiators — the very thing that negotiations are convened to overcome. For this reason, most negotiations, including union wage bargaining and environmental mediation, are conducted under agreements of privacy between the parties.

Second, the disclosure of options being considered early in the consultation process could easily cause hardship to bystanders, in a very unfair way. Early consultation must consider all possible options for the regulation or project being considered. Disclosure of options that are only being considered, and may not be included in any policy consensus reached by the negotiators, could be sufficient to disturb market values of assets potentially affected and cause unrest in communities and other undesirable social byproducts. This could prove damaging to individuals who would not otherwise be affected by the outcomes of the consultation.

The very sound arguments against confidentiality consist of all of the familiar reasons for the enactment of the U.S. Freedom of Information Act. In sum, citizens deserve to know what their government is doing. Important business should not be conducted in secrecy.

I believe that the deliberations of a consultative body should be available to the public, subject to the provisions of the Freedom of Information Act, as well as those of the Federal Advisory Committee Act, but with recognition of a few special circumstances.

The Freedom of Information Act refers specifically to documents and records. Any such written aspects of the ECS process would, by law, be available to the press and other interested parties. The Federal Advisory Committee Act provides that meetings of an advisory committee must be announced in the Federal Register at least ten days prior to the meeting. If a meeting is to be closed to the public, reasons for the closure must be given, and the name of an official designated to provide information about the meeting must be supplied. That information need not disclose details discussed in the meeting, but may be a summary of progress. It would seem reasonable that written material such as agendas, position summaries, and working papers used in meetings that have been declared closed by the ECS should be accorded the same confidential status. To make such a provision would be critical to the ability of ECS to conduct meaningful consultation.

While consultation is time consuming, it does not need to be nearly as delaying as referral to our crowded court system. Since parties to a consultative consensus, like the negotiators in the Pitch Mine case, seldom go to court, the use of an agency such as ECS should provide a considerable reduction in the average time it takes to actually put a regulation into effect or obtain final approval for a major project.

In summary then, I am proposing that Congress establish a consultative agency, with powers to review environmental regulations so that the views of diverse environmental stakeholders are considered in detail before regulations are adopted. The consultative agency (ECS) would not have the power to make decisions directly affecting regulation but would ensure that consultation adequately includes diverse viewpoints and technical expertise about the environment as they relate to each specific regulation. This agency would also provide consultation about major projects, government or private, affecting the environment.

Some time before resuming his role as administrator of the EPA, William Ruckelshaus commented about the Clean Air Act:

> What it [the nature of the Act] comes down to is that we are imposing on the American people a national program to improve the air which fails to take into account other legitimate social concerns . . . concerns no less legitimate than the air we breathe, for they also touch the very heart of the social fabric: the strength of our economy, our industrial productivity, our competitiveness in world markets. The regulatory process clearly ought to be in the public interest.[3]

If we really want our environmental protection programs to be in the public interest — in the interest of all the people of this country — then we must provide a way in which "other legitimate social concerns" can be included in the decision processes of our public servants. And this must be done at every level at which those decisions are made, not just in Congress. To do this, we will need to consult broadly with the stakeholders who know so well the parameters of those social concerns. This book has sought to outline the need and the rationale for such a consultative program. While my specific suggestions for accomplishing this are less important than would be a widespread awareness of the need for consultation (Americans know how to get things done, when they want to do them) still, I would hope that my ideas will point the way to a system that will rival those of the rest of the world in its fairness, its democracy, and its efficiency.

NOTES

1. _International Herald Tribune_, July 16, 1983, p. 9.

2. See, for example, International Labor Office, _Conciliation Services: Structures, Functions, and Techniques_ (Geneva:ILO, 1983).

3. William D. Ruckelshaus, in _Corporations and the Environment: How Should Decisions be Made?_, ed. David L. Brunner, Graduate School of Business, Stanford University, 1980, p. 166.

PART III
CASE STUDIES
OF ENVIRONMENTAL REGULATION

Introduction to the Case Studies

The cases, which constitute the remaining two chapters of this book, are real-life descriptions of regulatory situations. The first of the two describes the siting of a U.S. chemical plant and the problems that arise among the environmental stakeholders. The dilemmas that evolve are the result of both federal and state law — a condition always present in U.S. plant location. The second amplifies on the relationship between industry and government in Britain. It contains concrete examples of the cooperation described in Chapter 7.

The reader will be forgiven for suspecting that I have chosen these cases to prove a point, for certainly that is so. However, the cases are included here for an additional, and more important, reason. They represent the reality of environmental regulation! As both a teacher and a participant in the environmental process, I have learned that there is no better way, short of actual participation, to get a feeling for what happens in the day-to-day workings of the regulation of industry than through case studies. For this reason, I have tried to select cases that describe regulatory situations in an evenhanded way, without editorial comment. It is my hope that readers will draw their own conclusions from the material.

10
The Dow Chemical Company
California Project

On January 19, 1977, the Dow Chemical Company announced that it was dropping its plans to build a $500 million petrochemical complex in California. The company's press release indicated that managers had spent more than two years and $4 million in an attempt to obtain necessary permits to build the complex and cited excessive delays and costs in the permitting process as the major reason for terminating the project.

Because of subsequent investigations by the California legislature and attendant public statements by legislators and state regulatory employees, the public beyond the San Francisco Bay Area first became aware of the serious consequences of one of the major industry-environmental confrontations of the 1970's. The controversy was to grow among California lawmakers and regulators and spill over into the national scene, where it would augment pressure on the U.S. Environmental Protection Agency and Congress for modification of the Federal Clean Air Act.

At stake are not simply the technical requirements of the Clean Air Act, but the manner of interpretation of those requirements by federal, state, and local officers. Perhaps more importantly, what has come to be known as the "Dow Case" has called into question the entire bureaucratic process by which governmental agencies at various levels evaluate applications for permits to construct and operate industrial facilities.

This case, written by the author, was previously published in George A. Steiner and John F. Steiner, <u>Casebook for Business, Government & Society</u>, 2nd ed. (New York: Random House, 1980), pp. 47-60, adapted. Reprinted with permission.

The "process," it is claimed, is often rife with overlapping jurisdictions, conflicting laws, and widely differing interpretations of federal, state, and local laws, arrived at independently by various agencies. The experience of Dow and other industrial firms with the process has been characterized as being "too long, too costly, and too indefinite." Some have concluded with California State Senator John Holmdahl that for industry "the unwelcome sign is out."

A BUSINESS DECISION

The long and frustrating experience of the planners at Dow Chemical U.S.A. began with a rational decision to build a petrochemical complex near Collinsville in Solano County, California, on the Sacramento River. Dow executives viewed the proposed plant as an expansion of its Pittsburg, California, plant located on the San Joaquin River, in the Sacramento Delta 4.5 miles away. The purpose of the new facility would be to produce olefins and their derivatives which are basic feedstocks for a wide variety of chemical products consumed on the West Coast. Dow was supplying olefins from its Texas and Louisiana plants and would at decision time derive a $56 million annual saving in freight alone from West Coast production. Stanford Research Institute has estimated that by 1980 Dow would derive a $160 million annual freight saving. North Slope Alaskan oil was becoming available, and West Coast refineries were expected to produce an ample supply of naphtha (which together with salt would be Dow's basic raw material) for the company's needs. It was rumored that Dow marketers had their eyes on a 40 percent share of West Coast petrochemical demand.

The expansion called for construction of 13 production units, which were to be integrated and mutually supportive and were also to be integrated with the company's existing production facilities at Pittsburg. Land required for this expansion was about 800 acres. The company had only 200 acres of undeveloped land at its 450-acre Pittsburg site, and there was no additional land available in the area that could be purchased and would be suitable to accommodate the expansion. Because of this, the company acquired a site in Solano County, located directly across the San Joaquin and Sacramento Rivers from the company's Pittsburg site, and proposed to tie the two sites together with pipelines. The pipelines were to be buried beneath the river beds. The primary production mission of the Solano County plants would be to produce feedstocks to be delivered to the Pittsburg site via the underground pipelines.

The basic feedstocks for the new plants is naphtha, a low-grade form of gasoline produced from petroleum. Naphtha has an octane rating of about 30, compared to an octane rating of 90 that is required for an acceptable grade of gasoline. Conversion of refining facilities in the San Francisco area to nonleaded gasolines was expected to create substantial excess supplies of naphtha in the near future. This would create both an air pollution and a disposal problem unless facilities existed to convert this naphtha into products other than gasoline. Managers expected to be able to purchase the company's naphtha requirements from San Francisco area refineries and transport it by barge to the new production sites.

Dow planners had estimated that it would cost more than $500 million (in 1975 dollars) to construct the facilities over a five- to seven-year period. About 1,000 construction workers would be required to build the plants, and once completed they would be expected to provide 1,000 new permanent basic manufacturing jobs, 600 of these being in Contra Costa County and 400 of them in Solano County. These jobs would have an estimated annual payroll of $15 million. The facilities would increase the tax base in Contra Costa County by about 5 percent, and the tax base in Solano County would be increased by 14 percent.

The company's Pittsburg site was already zoned for heavy industrial use. The Solano County site chosen is a 2,700-acre parcel, which in 1971 was included in the Solano County general plan for water-oriented heavy industrial development. The land itself is isolated, remote marginal agricultural land located in rolling hills with elevations up to 250 feet. Dry farming practices are conducted in a three-year cycle. It produces grain one year, the second year it is used for sheep grazing on grain stubble, and it is allowed to lie fallow during the third year in this cycle. Value of the food and fiber products produced on the ranch is $70 per acre per year. This is considered to be the best agricultural use of this land. Before it was acquired by Dow, it had been advertised nationally for three years as an industrial plant site.

Dow proposed to utilize about 800 acres of this site, leaving the remaining 1,900 acres in a green belt zone, which would continue to be used for agricultural purposes.

The 13 units would include plants to produce styrene, ethylene, and propylene, and there would be a benzene unit. From there, Dow planned to move downstream to ethylbenzene, cumene, phenol, acetone, propylene oxide, and high- and low-density polyethylene. There would be caustic chlorine, and a vinyl chloride unit that could well become a target of the environmentalists.

The materials to be produced in the Dow plants were basic in the sense that they would find their way into a wide variety of end products such as soap, paper, insecticides, insulation, cleaning solvents, plywood, aluminum, steel, hospital equipment, furniture, and clothing, as well as auto bodies, boats, latex paint, kidney dialysis filters, plastic cups, brake fluid, and many others.

THE PERMIT PROCESS

Dow managers have years of experience in coping with the environmental exigencies of new plant construction. Dow had installed new facilities of comparable complexity to the proposed Collinsville operation in the United States and abroad in recent years. The new plants were expected to be complex, but not a difficult challenge. However, their concern for environmental regulation held a high priority from the start. In a published statement they claimed the following:

> Naturally, a project of this scope raises many questions. How will it affect the environment? What about air and water pollution? Who will get the jobs? Will taxes go up or down? Where will the new employees live? How will it benefit the economy? Will it trigger runaway economic growth, especially the kind that brings more problems than it solves?
>
> At Dow we gave a lot of thought to these questions before the project was proposed. Dow is a world-wide organization employing about 53,000 people. We enjoy the esteem of the business community because our employees are efficient, hard working, conscientious, and imaginative. Dow appreciates this respect from the business community, but above it we place the respect of our employees, the communities in which they reside and the people we serve. At Dow we do not cut corners — not on safety, not on quality, not on research, not on environmental controls. We value — highly value — our reputation as a responsible company and a good neighbor.

Managers at the corporation insist that the concerns expressed were genuine and that they still form a framework for the firm's operations around the world.

The permit process began informally in fall 1974 with private discussions between corporate officials and governmental agencies about the feasibility of the proposed operations. The sequence of events that followed between Dow and governmental agencies is shown in exhibit 1.

It was determined that 65 permits would be required from 12 federal, state, and local agencies. These are listed in exhibit 2.

In February 1975 the company concluded that a plant at Collinsville would be feasible and managers publicly announced plans for construction.

EXHIBIT 1

Chronology of Governmental and Public Consideration
of the Dow California Project

Fall of 1974	Dow officials met privately with local, regional, state and federal government agencies to discuss plans for proposed project.
February 1975	Public announcement of plans.
August–December 1975	Environmental Impact Report completed and approved by Contra Costa and Solano Counties after extensive public hearings. Portion of Solano County site rezoned general manufacturing.
December 1975	Sierra Club, Friends of the Earth, and People for Open Space filed petition in Solano County Superior Court asking for writ of mandate against Solano County for improper findings on EIR, cancelling part of Williamson Act contract and rezoning land.
January–April 1975	Applications for permits, easements, leases made to State agencies.
April 1976	Draft Environmental Statement published by U.S. Corps of Engineers for federal permits.
June 1976	Public hearing by Corps of Engineers. Secretary of State Resources Agency requested Corps to withhold approval of federal permits until State is satisfied with environmental impacts. State boards delay consideration of permit applications.
May 1976	Comments received on Draft Environmental Statement from interested persons.
July 1976	Application for permit to Bay Area Pollution Control District for construction of styrene plant.
August 1976	Denial of styrene permit by Bay Area Air Pollution Control Officer. Appeal to Hearing Board initiated by Dow. Hearings started September 16.
December 1976	Hearings for five state agencies on environmental effects of project convened by State Office of Planning and Research.
January 19, 1977	Dow withdraws from project.

131

EXHIBIT 2
Dow California Project
Summary of Permits Required

Federal	Purpose	Number Required	Total
U.S. Corps of Engineers	a) Dock and ship turning basin	1	1
	b) Water intake	1	1
	c) Water discharge	1	1
	d) Pipeline crossing	1	1
U.S. Coast Guard	a) Transport (operational) over dock	1	1
Subtotal (Federal)			5

State	Purpose	Number Required	Total
Regional Water Board	a) NPDES for osmosis reject	1*	1*
	b) NPDES for water return on dredging spoils	1	1
	c) Certificate of Conformance	1	1
	d) Evaporation ponds	1 ea. pond	2**
	e) Sanitary treatment (even if no discharge)	1	1
	f) Storm water run-off from land maintained in agricultural use	1	1
Water Resources Control Board	a) Appropriative Water Rights	1	1
Department of Water Resources	a) Dam Safety	1	1
Fish and Game	a) Alteration of stream bed for dock, water intake, and pipelines	1 ea.	3
Reclamation Board	a) Alter levees	1	1
State Lands Commission	a) Lease for easements across state lands for dock, pipelines, and water intake	1	1
Bay Area Air Pollution Control District	a) Construction	1 ea. plant	13***
	b) Operation	1 ea. plant	13***
Subtotal (California)			40

Counties	Purpose	Number Required	Total
Sacramento	a) Use permit for pipelines	1	1
Solano	a) Building	1 ea. plant	7
	b) Sanitary	1	1
	c) Potable water	1	1
	d) Grading	1	1
	e) Use permit for pipelines	1	1
Contra Costa	a) Building	1 ea. plant	6
	b) Grading	1	1
	c) Use permit for pipelines	1	1
Subtotal (Counties)			20
Grand Total			65

*Obtained September 26, 1975.
**Absolute minimum number of ponds is two.
***Absolute minimum since each plant has at least one vent.

California law requires the designation of a "lead agency" to evaluate the impact of any project such as Dow's, and upon request the Governor's Office of Planning and Research designated Solano County as that agency. The same office also designated Contra Costa County as a "party of special interest." Contra Costa was asked to participate in the environmental impact report (EIR) review process, to conduct its own hearings, make legal findings of adequacy, and to advise Solano County of its conclusions.

Solano County, faced with the need for a massive EIR, and lacking the expertise in such matters, went to J. B. Gilbert and Associates, a consulting firm in Sacramento specializing in this type of work. Dow agreed to pay Gilbert's fee. Environmentalists were later to refer consistently to the report as "Dow's EIR," not Solano County's.

After preparation of the report, Solano County began its consideration of the impact of Dow's project in September 1975. Copies of the report were sent to interested parties with requests for comments. Nicholas Arguimbau, attorney for the Sierra Club and the Environmental Defense Fund, recalls that they had to move rapidly. The Environmental Defense Fund did not receive its draft copy of the EIR until September 11. The County Planning Commission requested comments by September 18. On September 16 the EDF asked for a time extension, but hearings were held as planned, and on November 4 the county commissioners approved the EIR.

In December the Sierra Club, Friends of the Earth, and People for Open Space jointly filed suit against Solano County's planning commission, its board of supervisors, and the county itself. They asked that the permit process be halted, and they charged that the EIR did not adequately consider all of the environmental problems related to the proposed new plants.

Upon approval of the EIR by the county, Dow paid $230,000 in Williamson Act contract cancellation fees to the state of California, and the county rezoned 834 acres of Dow's site from agricultural to industrial. California's Williamson Act provides for a ten-year tax break to farmers if they promise to keep their land in agriculture; however, the contract may be abrogated if back taxes and certain fees are paid to the state. Dow also negotiated agreements with the county regarding the maintenance of roads leading to the site during the construction period.

Following Solano County's approval, Dow managers filed applications for the state permits required (see exhibit 2) and began the federal environmental review process. This latter process is necessary to the federal permits indicated in exhibit 2. The federal process was conducted by the U.S. Army Corps of Engineers (the permit-issuing agency) and required the approval of the

U.S. Environmental Protection Agency. The federal Environmental Impact Statement was completed and circulated by the Corps of Engineers in April 1976.

In May 1976 Dow submitted an application to the Bay Area Air Pollution Control District (APCD) for authorization to construct the first unit of the complex, a $50 million plant to convert ethylbenzene to styrene. To complete construction of all 13 units, Dow needed 26 permits from the District. The District advised Dow that each unit must be treated as a separate plant and that a permit to construct and a permit to operate are required for each plant. Further, the District advised that substantial construction must be underway within two years after each permit is granted. Each application requires a detailed description of the plant including storage tanks, all emission points, and all emission control equipment. The styrene plant has 14 emission points, one of which is assigned to fugitive losses from pumps, valves, and other seals. Dow's engineering included careful consideration of each emission point and specification of effective control equipment.

The analysis of the application by the District's engineers resulted in their conclusion that all emissions were less than the District's requirements.

Dispersion calculations were then made to obtain values for ground-level concentrations of the emitted materials to determine whether these concentrations were deemed to be "significant."

The District's regulations contain the following section:

> The Air Pollution Control officer shall deny any authority to construct . . . any facility . . . which may cause the emission or creation of a significant quantity of any air contaminant which would interfere with the attainment or maintenance of any air quality standard . . . anywhere in the District.

The regulation has not defined "significant quantity." The air pollution control officer and his staff have adopted a criterion of "significance" in considering permit applications. The criterion is that a quantity of emission is a "significant quantity" if the dispersion calculations predict that it will result in a ground-level concentration that could be detected by air-monitoring instrumentation. For example, the instrument detection level for nonmethane hydrocarbons is stated to be 0.20 parts per million (ppm.), for particulate, 5 ug per cubic meter, and so on.

In the case of combined sources, the several emission points and area sources are analyzed individually, and significance is achieved when the sum of the individual contributions exceeds the instrument sensitivity of detection.

The calculations of this Cmax showed that the Dow plant would emit significant quantities of hydrocarbon, NO_X, SO_2, and particulate.

Once the quantity of emissions has been determined, the staff must ascertain whether the emissions will interfere with the attainment or maintenance of air quality standards. In the case where standards are exceeded or will be at the time of proposed source operation in the area affected by a significant emission, a recommendation to deny the permit is made by the staff.

The staff has determined that the Montezuma Hills area (the site location) in Solano County exceeds standards on several days per year for particulate, hydrocarbons, and oxidant. Thus, the permit was denied. Although the NO_X and SO_2 emissions were found to be in significant quantities, the standards were said not to be exceeded in the area for these materials.

Dow says the styrene plant is a very clean plant and very low in emissions. The NO_X, SO_2, and particulate are due to the burning of fuel for the reactor. Eighty-three percent of the fuel is gas, and the remaining 17 percent is oil or liquid process residue hydrocarbons. The emission values for fuel burning were assigned values from the EPA compilation AP-42. In some cases there are ranges given in AP-42, such as a range of 5 to 15 pounds of particulate per million standard cubic feet of gas burned. In such a case, the District assigns the highest number, that is, 15. The hydrocarbons are emitted from the burning of fuel, storage tanks, and process hardware. The average total hydrocarbon emissions is 5 pounds per hour. The District uses the instantaneous maximum emission of 13.5 pounds per hour, which can occur at a time of unloading a ship, which is about one day of each 45 days. This piling up of all worst possible conditions into the same time period is justified by the District on the basis that the standard must not be exceeded under the worst possible conditions, not once per year.

Dow managers felt the permit was denied by the air pollution control officer on the basis of a very restrictive definition of "significant quantity" and of the federal and state ambient air quality standards.

The air pollution control officer told Dow that under present regulations there is no way he could grant a permit. He said the requirements of the EPA determined his decision, and the only remedy he could suggest was to persuade Congress to amend the Clean Air Act. Dow's response was to initiate an appeal of the permit denial with the hearing board of the Bay Air Pollution Control District.

Dow also disagreed with the conclusion of the San Francisco air pollution control officer that "detectability" has to take place inside the plant instead of at the plant boundary, as is recommended by EPA. Historically, Dow says, a plant's impact on ambient air quality has always been considered to take place at the plant boundary, where it affects air space to which the general public is exposed. Industrial hygiene standards (OSHA) have applied to the air environment in the plant. Dow believes that it can meet the detectability test being used by the air pollution control officer if it is applied at the boundary line.

The control officer, D. J. Callaghan, in an interview with the _Chemical and Engineering News_, agreed that the styrene plant was a clean one. Callaghan said, holding his thumb and forefinger a few millimeters apart, "It was this close." But in August he turned it down. "I was the only one to make a decision. Unfortunately it was a negative decision. I had no other choice."

The corporation had also sponsored private studies of the air quality impact. These were conducted by Stanford Research Institute (SRI). The efforts cast the project in a favorable light. The work involved the use of mathematical simulation modeling to assess the effects of proposed Dow operations on 1980 air quality. The study focused on ozone (O_3) concentrations because various earlier work had shown that O_3 was most likely to exceed the current ambient air quality standards. The analysis was based on the projection of air quality observed on six "trajectory days" selected from 1973 and included a projection with and without the Dow plants in 1980. The six days were selected because they represented particularly poor air quality as well as for other factors relating to the movement of air masses incident to the Dow site. The results of the study show that the proposed Dow facilities were unlikely to aggravate the ozone problem. Table 10.1 actually shows small predicted reductions in ozone concentrations on several of the chosen days. It should be noted, however, that with one exception the predicted values on each "trajectory day" for 1980 exceeded the ambient air quality standard for ozone, which is 80 parts per billion. SRI scientists explain this surprising result in the following way:

> The seemingly unusual result that the emissions from the Dow facilities will actually decrease (rather than increase) downwind ozone concentrations comes about because the expected emissions of nitric oxide (NO) will be large relative to those of non-methane hydrocarbons (NMHC). The ratio of nitrogen exides (NO_X) to NMHC in an air mass is a critical factor controlling the formation of ozone. The Dow emissions will be added to ambient air which already has an NO_X/NMHC concentration ratio that is about 0.5. In order for added NO to produce ozone within a few hours, the NO_X/NMHC ratio must be considerably smaller than this. Thus in this case, the main effect of the

TABLE 10.1
Summary of Projected Peak-Hour
Ozone Concentrations (parts per billion)

Test No.	Date of Meteorologicals and Air Quality Conditions Used	1973 Observed	1973 Calculated	1980 Projected without Dow Emissions	1980 Projected with Dow Emssions
1	May 17, 1973	83	94	87	86
2	June 21, 1973 (A)	156	122	144	133
3	June 21, 1973 (B)	160	115	133	119
4	July 26, 1973	160	121	138	138
5	July 27, 1973	63	92	112	111
6	August 14, 1973	83	75	59	59

<u>Note</u>: Ambient air quality standard is 80 parts per billion.

added NO is to convert ozone to oxygen through the following reaction:

$$NO + O_3 \longrightarrow NO_2 + O_2$$

This effect is well known to atmospheric scientists and is commonly observed for considerable distances downwind of major NO sources such as power plants and freeway interchanges.

Early in 1975 the company planners had made application to several state agencies for permits, leases, and easements. At the time of Dow's troubles with the Air Pollution Control District, permits were pending before the Reclamation Board, Water Resources Control Board, and Department of Water Resources. Lease applications and easement requests had been made to the Fish and Game Department and State Lands Commission.

Several of these agencies were uncertain about their authority in interpreting the EIR as it related to the function of the agencies. Dow managers had in fact determined that the secretary of the Resources Agency had asked the Corps of Engineers to withhold decisions on all federal permits until the state was satisfied with concerns that it had about the project.

Thus, by the fall of 1976, Dow managers had achieved the approval of the project EIR by Solano County and had arranged for the associated easement and road requirements. A total of four permits had been issued, and the company's land had been rezoned. Dow had struck out with Air Pollution Control District (and was appealing its case), was moving slowly with state agencies, and federal permits were on the back burner. Managers calculated they would need a total of 65 permits to finish the job, and the prospects were growing dimmer.

PROS AND CONS

Public interest and involvement with the project had been growing steadily, and by late 1976 the list of organizations involved in regulation, or lending support to one side or the other, was quite impressive. _San Francisco Magazine_ counted 81 such groups (see Appendix 10.1).

Dow drew major support from the counties of Solano and Contra Costa, the Contra Costa Taxpayers Association, the Bay Area Coalition of Labor and Business, and organized labor in the form of the State Building and Construction Trades Council. These groups saw the benefit of jobs, trade, and an expanded tax base as paramount considerations.

Supporting the other side of the issue were environmental forces led by the Sierra Club, Friends of the Earth, and People for Open Space. Their arguments focused on potential damage to the environment. While almost every possible environmental issue was discussed, several major problems occupied the center stage throughout "the process." These major issues together with the responses of Dow Chemical are as follows:

1. The opposition charged that the EIR was inadequate to assess the impact on the environment. The California Environmental Quality Act required the EIR to fully describe the expected impact of the project on "land, air, water, minerals, flora, fauna, ambient noise, and objects of historic or aesthetic significance." Dow defended the EIR as follows:

The Environmental Impact Report that has been prepared for this project is one of the most thorough and extensive ever prepared for any major project conceived in California. It cost $750,000 and more than 30 consultants, all leading experts in their field, participated in its preparation.

It was the subject of numerous public hearings and reviews in both Solano and Contra Costa counties. All state agencies and local government groups with an interest in the project commented extensively on the report, as did many public interest groups, school classes, and private citizens. Responses to all their questions and comments were prepared, reviewed and published before the reports were legally certified by both counties as an adequate assessment of the significant environmental, social and economic impacts of the project.

This process covered an 18 month period and was necessary before Dow could apply for the 70 different government permits that it must obtain before the project can be completed. Certain federal permits are also required and the entire state environmental review process must be duplicated at the federal level before the federal permits can be obtained. This federal review process is now underway.

Environmental laws require that only the possible bad or adverse impacts of any project be reviewed and assessed. Environmental Impact Report writers must describe the worst possible situation that could conceivably happen, even if the situation is only a hypothetical one. They ignore any good impacts.

The Environmental Impact Report on the Dow project weighs four pounds, and it covers every subject that the experience and imagination of man can conceive, from air, water and solid waste impacts to transportation, taxes, housing, agriculture, highways, schools, the economy, every area plant and animal species from birds to field mice.

The plants Dow wants to build will have zero water pollution like our Pittsburg plant. They will have zero solid waste pollution. Air emissions will be well within any standard that is required.

2. It was charged that the Dow plant would withdraw valuable agricultural land from farming uses. The Sierra Club claims that the Williamson Act contract was broken illegally, and that Solano County violated its general plan when it zoned 834 acres for industrial use. The Dow management responded:

The plant site is presently used for dry farming. It produces barley and sheep. Historically it has provided a modest living for farm families. The land, by all standards, is marginal agricultural land.

The Solano County general plan designated the area several years ago as one that it wanted to be used for industrial development.

The land presently produces less than $70 worth of agricultural products per acre per year. These yields are less than 1/4th of one percent of the average productivity of agricultural land in California. And the farming practices employed there are judged by all experts as being the best use that can be made of this land if it is used for agricultural purposes.

Dow estimates that more than $50 million of products will be produced each year by its proposed new plants which will have both a direct and an indirect benefit for agriculture in California.

3. There was concern that the entire area might be converted to an industrial complex if Dow were allowed to build. Opponents used the term the "Ruhr Valley of California" to describe their expectations for the area. In fact, Arco Chemical had announced plans to build a petrochemical plant roughly twice the size of Dow's proposed operation on an adjacent site. They had also been denied a permit by the APCD. In addition, National Steel as well as Pacific Gas and Electric either owned or had optioned land nearby. Dow claimed:

The Dow project does not depend upon other industrial development of the area. Our customers are already using the projects we will produce. The only difference will be that we will produce them in California instead of on the Gulf Coast.

What other companies do in the future will be determined by them and the decisions of Solano and Contra Costa County officials, as well as the multilayered and complex system of government agencies. They control the pace, style and type of development that occurs anywhere. Both counties, as well as the regional, state and federal government entities, have well trained, competent staffs.

If other industries do locate in the area, we hope they will be required to meet the same high standards that are being required of Dow.

4. Opponents feared that since the plant would be located in the path of marine air blowing through the Carquinez Strait, this major source of fresh air for California's agriculturally rich Central Valley basin would be seriously polluted. Some experts believe that wind conditions and inversion heights made the basin a candidate for worse air pollution than the Los Angeles basin. It was claimed that because of these potential problems any addition of pollution to the atmosphere would be intolerable. Dow managers assessed the air pollution problem as follows:

Dow's proposed plants will utilize the latest and best air control technology in the world. Many technological improvements have been made in recent years which are impractical or too costly to use in older plants but which can be designed into new plants today.

If our plants cannot be designed to meet air standards, we will not be able to get permits to build them.

Will we be able to eliminate all air emissions? No one has been able to accomplish this. But we keep trying.

5. The 55,000-acre Suisun Marsh is located a few miles downstream from Dow's proposed site. Some 202 species of birds and 26 mammal types live there. The marsh is also the wintering grounds for birds moving along the Pacific Flyway. The southern bald eagle and the perigrin falcon, both endangered species, inhabit the area. Critics warned that chemical spills from Dow manufacturing or shipping operations could devastate the marsh as well as threaten the king salmon, striped bass, and sturgeon indigenous to the Sacramento River. According to Dow:

The marsh is a very tender and fragile wildlife resource and the possibility that our plants might have some impact on this area was the subject of much and careful thought before the Solano County site was selected. The marsh already has a number of industrial neighbors, located either adjacent to it or across the river. Many ships carrying chemicals and other products have been traversing the Sacramento River Channel in front of the marsh for years enroute to Stockton and Sacramento ports and to industrial locations in the Delta area. Dow ship traffic will be about three ships or barges per week. Damage to the marsh from Dow's operations, if it occurred, would have to be from chemical spills caused by ship collisions in front of the marsh or upstream, or from the possibility of accidental spills at the Dow dock during loading and unloading operations. Recognizing this possibility, Dow developed one of the most sophisticated spill prevention and containment plans ever devised. It calls for three lines of defense to contain spills at the dock if they occur, and a system of mobile booms, skimmer boats and other facilities to protect environmentally sensitive points throughout the Delta, not just the marsh. The chemical materials Dow will be handling evaporate within six hours, should a spill occur. Studies of tides, current and winds, and ship traffic in the Delta and Bay area enable us to determine where spilled materials will go under any conditions that may exist at the time of an accident. This knowledge will enable us to get ahead of the spill and protect sensitive areas.

Dow has been shipping chemicals past the marsh for more than 38 years. The only spill that occurred during that time happened at our Pittsburg plant dock. It involved a spill of 50 gallons. It was quickly contained at the dock.

6. Neither the EIR or the EIS specifically state the level of vinyl chloride emissions to be expected from the plant. Both lump all hydrocarbon emissions together. Opponents pointed out that the Texas Air Control Board estimates vinyl chloride emissions from Dow's Freeport Texas plant at 16.3 tons per day. Dow has contended that those figures are out of date and that emissions from the new plant will be very small. Dow's statement about vinyl chloride was:

Dow has been producing vinyl chloride for many years. There has never been one single case of cancer detected in a Dow employee that was related to work in a vinyl chloride plant. Dow has been monitoring the health of its employees since it established research laboratories in the 1930's to study the health effects associated with the use or production of chemical substances. The health of Dow employees who work every day in chemical plants throughout the world is significantly better than the national averages and the incidence of cancer is much lower than national averages.

About 15 years ago Dow urged the government to set a safe exposure for workers in vinyl chloride plants. Dow studies had indicated that a safe level — one that Dow used in its plants — was 50 parts per million. The government did set a standard, but it was 500 parts per million instead of 50. Dow continued to use its own 50 parts per million standards.

Last year, because of publicity about vinyl chloride plants and cancer caused by conditions that existed 30 years ago, the exposure standard was reduced to one part per million — 50 times the known safe level of exposure.

Today all Dow plants, as well as vinyl chloride plants operated by other producers, comply with the one part per million standard. If they don't comply, the government shuts them down.

7. Ship and barge traffic up the Sacramento Channel would have increased because of the Dow plant (critics claimed the traffic would double). The EIR states that after completion of the plant there would be an "18 fold increase over the 1973 total tonnage of hazardous material transported on the Sacramento River." Opponents were concerned about the possibility of spills of dangerous material and the consequent threat to life and health in the area. Dow managers said this about their water operations:

> An analysis of water shipments and accidents in the nation show that the probability of an accident involving a Dow ship in the Delta is one in every 40 years. These statistical odds, however, ignore technological advances that have been made in very recent years in the field of marine accident prevention and clean up techniques.
>
> A study of the 65 marine accidents which have occurred in the Bay Area's waters from all shipping, including the Delta, during the last eight years indicated only three actually resulted in spills of materials into the water. None of these collisions involved spills of materials being transported by Dow.
>
> Very elaborate facilities have been designed to prevent or contain accidental spills at the Dow dock.
>
> Even the four pipelines which will be constructed below the Sacramento Riverbed will be designed to minimize danger of rupture in the event of earthquakes.

THE HEARINGS

As the arguments grew more heated, Dow managers became more concerned about the possibility of ultimate failure for their project. At a meeting with Governor Edmund Brown, Jr., they complained of the delays and government red tape that were holding up the project. According to Bill Press, director of the Governor's Office of Planning and Research, Brown's only assurance at that meeting was that Dow would get a fair hearing. However, as a result of the meeting, Press agreed to set up a special hearing at which Dow managers and representatives of five interested state agencies would be present. The idea according to Dow personnel was to get all of the relevant questions asked once and for all and then get started with the issuance of permits, where appropriate. Contrary to Press's statements about the governor's commitment, Dow managers have insisted that the governor agreed to definite time limitations for state action and to a specific format for the hearing.

The consolidated hearings were set for December 8 and 9, 1976. They were later extended to include December 17. The participants were to be Dow Chemical Company, the State Reclamation Board, the State Water Resources Control Board, the State Lands Commission, and the Department of Water Resources, together with such witnesses and other interested parties as each might call.

Three significant events were to occur before the hearings convened. First, on November 5 Bill Press wrote to Ray Brubaker, Dow's western division manager, enclosing a list of questions to which various state agencies would like answers at the hearings. Seventy-six separate questions were included in the list. It is included here as Appendix 10.2. In his letter, Press said in part:

> These questions reflect the concerns of state agencies which may be raised at the hearing. I am submitting them to you as early as possible, so that you and your representatives will be fully prepared to respond to them at the December hearing. You may choose to submit written responses to the questions in advance to assist evaluation of the project.

Second, on November 16 the State Water Resources Control Board wrote to the state attorney general requesting legal clarification of the California Environmental Quality Act (CEQA). The board asked "What alternative procedural and substantive steps can responsible agencies take to ensure compliance with CEQA prior to taking final action on the project?"

The attorney general's response was to come on December 7, just one day before the hearings were to commence. In the opinion of his staff:

> The lead agency principle does not exempt agencies from the requirement of CEQA. It only excuses them from the

duty of preparing an EIR when another public agency has prepared an EIR on the project. The lead agency principle is designed to prevent duplication of paperwork. It is not to be used as a device to avoid the basic responsibilities under the act.

and:

The need for the concurrence of all responsible agencies in the adequacy of an EIR reflects the independent obligation of all public agencies to comply with CEQA.

In summary, the letter advised the state agencies that they were not required to accept the lead agency's (Solano County) EIR, that each agency must satisfy itself independently of the environmental prudence of issuing permits, and if deemed appropriate each agency should supplement or modify the EIR for its purpose. It also advised that state agencies could rely on the federal Environmental Impact Statement for the project if they deemed that document adequate. The determination of adequacy would be left to the agencies individually.

Third, on November 30 the State Reclamation Board issued revised guidelines for testimony and the qualifications of participants in the hearings. The original notice of hearing was issued by the State Water Resources Control Board. It stated in part:

Oral testimony will be taken under oath, witnesses will be subject to cross-examination by the hearing panel and the proceedings will be recorded by a court reporter.

and:

On or before November 24, 1976, those intending to participate in this hearing shall submit to the Office of Planning and Research at the above address, in writing, the name of each witness who will testify for them, together with a statement of the qualifications of each expert witness, the subject of the proposed testimony and the estimated time required by the witness to present his or her direct testimony. Preference in allotting speaking time shall be given to those notifying the Office of Planning and Research on or before November 24. Copies of proposed exhibits or testimony submitted in advance will, to the extent practical, be reproduced and made available to the hearing panel. Any written evidence submitted by December 23 will be made a part of the record.

The November 30 notice referred to testimony only as follows:

> The purpose of this hearing is to afford Dow Chemical Company, Inc., state and local agencies, and the public, an opportunity to present relevant oral and written evidence on the potential environmental and economic impacts, both beneficial and adverse, of the proposed plant.

The effect of this revision, Dow managers claim, was to convert the hearings from a technical proceeding where "expert witnesses" would present sworn testimony for the record, subject to cross-examination, to a public forum. In this latter mode, Dow claims, nearly anyone who wished to make a statement about the project, factual or otherwise, could be heard.

The hearings proceeded for three days. The transcript covers 1,200 pages.

Following the hearings, on January 3, 1977, Bill Press wrote to Arthur M. Shelton, counsel for Dow, requesting further information required by state agencies. He indicated that responses when submitted "will be used by state agencies to formally supplement the Dow EIR prepared by Solano County."

The material that Press conveyed with his letter contained 134 additional questions raised by state agencies. Twenty-nine of these were requests for additional material relevant to questions asked at the hearings — material that Dow's managers had agreed to provide. The balance of the questions covered essentially new subject matter. Included were questions from five state agencies (see Appendix 10.2) not previously publicly identified as interested in the Dow project and from whom permits were not required. These agencies are the State Air Resources Board, the Department of Food and Agriculture, the Department of Health, the Solid Waste Management Board, and the Seismic Safety Commission.

On January 19 Dow made its announcement that it would withdraw the project, citing continued delays in the involved permitting process and its need to act promptly to assure production facilities to meet future demand. According to Paul Oreffice, Dow's president, "In the final analysis, what killed us was the uncertainty."

However, at least one participant in the process felt that Dow's decision to withdraw was a satisfactory one. In its official newspaper, New Man Apart, Friends of the Earth headlined a story about the Dow project, "Can a quiet agricultural county on the Sacramento River find true happiness with a huge messy chemical plant?"

APPENDIX 10.1

Organizations and Localities Involved
in the California "Dow Issue"

Federal
U.S. Army Corps of
  Engineers*
Department of Agriculture
Department of Commerce
Department of Health,
  Education and Welfare
Department of Housing and
  Urban Development
Department of the Interior
Department of
  Transportation
Coast Guard
Environmental Protection
  Agency*
Federal Energy
  Administration*

State
Governor's office: Office of
  Planning and Research*
Attorney general's office*
State Resources Agency*
Air Resources Board*
Department of Fish and
  Game*
Department of Food and
  Agriculture*
Department of Health*
Employment Development
  Department
Seismic Safety Commission*
State Lands Commission*

Solid Waste Management
  Board*
State Water Resources
  Control Board*

Regional
Association of Bay Area
  Governments
Bay Area Air Pollution
  Control District*
Bay Conservation and
  Development Commission

County
Solano County
  Board of Supervisors*
  Planning Commission*
  Planning Department*
  Industrial Development
  Agency*
Contra Costa County
Sacramento County

Cities
Antioch
Benicia
Davis
Fairfield
Pittsburg
Rio Vista
Vacaville
Vallejo

Appendix 10.1, cont.

Private Organizations

American Indian Movement
Associated General
  Contractors of California
Associated Students,
  University of California,
  Davis
Audubon Society
Benicia Industries Council
California Advisory
  Commission on Marine and
  Coastal Resources
California Chamber of
  Commerce
California Coordinating
  Council
California Inland Pilots
  Association
California Lung Association
California Trout
California Water Fowl
  Association
Coalition of Labor and
  Business
Committee for Preservation
  of Agricultural Lands in
  Solano
Contra Costa County
  Affirmative Action Council
Contra Costa County Park
  Council
Delta Advisory Council
Environmental Defense Fund
Farmers of Winters
Friends of the Earth

Friends of the River
Landowners of Collinsville
League of Women Voters
National Wildlife Federation
The Nature Conservancy
Northern California
  Committee for
  Environmental Information
Oceanic Society
Oil, Chemical and Atomic
  Workers International Union
Operating Engineers Local
  No. 3
People for Open Space
Rio Vista Chamber of
  Commerce
Save Florida
Save San Francisco Bay
  Association
Sierra Club
Solano Citizens Access to
  Planning
Solano County Committee for
  Environmental Action
Solano County Taxpayers
  Association
State Building and
  Construction Trades Council
Student Democratic Council
Students for Environmental
  Action
West Contra Costa
  Conservation League

*Key agencies
Source: San Francisco magazine

APPENDIX 10.2

Questions for Consolidated State Agency Hearing
on Dow's Proposed Petrochemical Facility

(These questions reflect the concerns that have been raised to
date by various state agencies that have permit or review authority over the project. Other issues may be raised at the
hearing.)

A. <u>WATER QUALITY AND CHEMICAL SPILLS</u>
   1. For each chemical or mixture to be transported, what
      common or technical names are used to identify them?
      What is the anticipated range of variation and composi-
      tion of mixtures such as naphtha? Exactly which chlor-
      othylenes will be produced and transported?
   2. Is it feasible to convert the proposed plant to the manu-
      facture of other chemicals than those identified in the
      EIR, draft EIS, and spill plan? Is such conversion
      planned? Is any expansion planned or likely that would
      alter the output of the proposed plant?
   3. For each chemical or mixture to be transported, what
      physical or chemical properties may affect spill dis-
      persion and impact, toxicity to humans, toxicity to ani-
      mals, toxicity to plants, toxicity to aquatic life, hazards
      to the public, and effectiveness of countermeasures
      designed to mitigate spills or releases? What other
      adverse effects on fish and wildlife, including water as-
      sociated mammals and birds and their habitats, have been
      identified? Would any of the chemicals or chemical
      components transported be soluble in water, and if so,
      could they enter surface soils and have long lasting
      sublethal effects on aquatic vegetation, aquatic life, or
      wildlife?
   4. For each chemical or mixture to be transported, what
      deleterious effects or undesirable properties have been
      reported in the literature available through standard
      computerized indexes of the chemical and medical
      literature?
   5. Are any of the chemicals or mixtures associated with
      carcinogenesis industrial disease syndromes, toxicity,
      deleterious effects produced by exposure to small
      amounts of the materials, such as hormonal effects on
      plants, spontaneous explosive polymerization, corrosivity,
      or formation of hazardous products under the influence
      of fire?
   6. For each chemical or mixture to be transported, what
      methods of transportation will be used? What range of

volumes will be transported by each method? What volume of material will be capable of being released into the environment at each stage of each transportation sequence?

7. For each chemical or mixture, what are the anticipated shipment volumes, annual amounts to be transported, amounts per shipment by type of shipment container, dilution or physical state during shipment, expected product destinations, and expected use at point of delivery?

8. Where a number of markets are available or a raw material can be obtained from a number of sources, what alternatives are available for source or market locations, shipment methods, and exposure of sensitive areas to spill hazards during transportation?

9. Estimates should be provided using methods other than that given in the spill plan of the risks of spills or accidental releases of materials during transport for anticipated water, truck, and rail transport of each chemical.

10. What are the probabilities of spills from ship accidents calculated from available information for San Francisco Bay, the delta, and available predications of increased ship traffic during the life of the proposed project, including those of the U.S. Army Corps of Engineers?

11. What are the expected ship traffic increases associated with industrial development of the Montezuma Hills area, increased traffic to Bay Area oil refineries, proposed modifications of the San Francisco, Stockton, and Baldwin Ship Channels, and increased small boat traffic from recreational expansion in the delta?

12. What degree of intrusion and environmental effect on the Suisun Marsh can be expected from a "worst case" spill occurring along the line of the proposed transportation route, from tank car spills along the proposed rail line and existing rail lines, and from tank trucks along the portions of transportation routes passing through watersheds tributary to the marsh? If such spills were to occur what would be the solubility, volatility, and flammability of each material that could reach the Suisun Marsh or any part of the San Francisco Bay system?

13. What releases of materials are possible from pipeline breaks for the propylene oxide, chloroethylene, ethylene, propylene, and hydrogen pipelines identified in the draft EIR, draft EIS, and spill plan?

14. What volumes may be released, at what locations are releases possible, what vulnerable situations are located

along pipeline routes, and what safeguards are available to prevent significant releases from pipeline ruptures? If a pipeline rupture should occur, what emergency plans and measures are proposed to warn the domestic water suppliers (City of Antioch and Contra Costa County Water District) utilizing the receiving waters for domestic use? What means of construction will be employed to minimize or eliminate the threat of future pipeline ruptures?

15. What releases may be expected from rupture of a typical individual transportation compartment when materials are transported by each of the following methods: barge, tanker, tank truck, and tank car?

16. What range of volumes of potential releases is determined by the available range of expected transportation vehicles? What release volume can be expected from rupture of two adjacent compartments? What release volume can be expected from loss of an entire cargo? What is the nature and likelihood of an event necessary to produce a release of each size category?

17. What forms of life and resources along proposed transportation routes are particularly vulnerable to the effects of releases of the chemicals or mixtures to be transported?

18. What possibilities for permanent or long-lasting damage can be identified for the Suisun Marsh, including cases where spill probabilities are low, but the consequences of a spill event are serious and significant?

19. What effective countermeasures are available for each type of spill identified? Are nonstructural countermeasures available, such as scheduling, avoidance of unfavorable tide and current conditions, avoidance of particularly hazardous routes, or avoidance of transport during the seasonal presence of migrating species, as significant mitigation measures for spill hazards?

20. The Merck Index states that ethylene dichloride is soluble in about 120 parts water. How long would this material be expected to remain in a pool directly under the point of release, as described on page 17 of the spill plan? What would be the effect of an ethylene dichloride spill on benthic organisms? How long could ethylene dichloride be expected to remain localized under the influence of river currents?

21. What would be the distribution of deleterious effects to beneficial uses of water resulting from "worst-case" spills of each of those chemicals to be transported? Analysis of "worst-case" spills should include:

    a. Consideration of a series of locations from spills covering those areas where spills are most likely or where they would exert the greatest deleterious effects on sensitive environmental features;

    b. Those combinations of river flow rate, tidal conditions, and seasonal presence of vulnerable migrating species that would produce maximum deleterious effects;

    c. Maximum upstream and downstream transportation of spilled materials possible under adverse combinations of spill conditions, tidal stage, and river flow;

    d. The location and volume of water that would be affected.

    Where a large, continuous range of possible conditions exist, the discussions should clearly identify the extreme cases and should indicate the range of the most probable sets of conditions to be expected.

22. What are the adverse impacts on beneficial water uses resulting from potential accidental chemical spills involving the largest quantity of chemicals possible from the mode of transportation under "worst-case" conditions?

23. What are the limitations of the spill containment equipment that would be deployed in the proposed dock area Collinsville and in the Sacramento River? If boom facilities are to be deployed, what are the difficulties encountered in this type of containment procedure?

24. What will be the shape and extent of the initial mixing zone around the outfall structure and diffuser when under the influence of various tidal conditions? What tests will be conducted on storm water in production areas to determine whether it meets sufficient water quality standards to be discharged into the river?

B. HAZARDOUS WASTE DISPOSAL

1. What are the quantities and chemical composition of the Class I wastes expected to be generated by the proposed facility (including those produced by processes such as quenching, cracking, distillation, oxidation, acidification, and hydrodeakylation)? How will such wastes be disposed of? What will be the composition and volume of spent catalysts? How will they be disposed of?

2. Where will such wastes be disposed? How long will the proposed disposal site be usable?

3. What disposal options exist for Class I wastes? What types of organic materials will be included in these

wastes, and how will their presence affect the possibility of disposal through controlled incineration? What will be the chemical composition, volume, and general nature of wastes that will be put in evaporation ponds?

4. What materials have been observed in the Class I wastes generated by similar chemical synthesis plants?

5. What are the impacts of the discharge of dissolved solids (for example, chromate and chromium) to land adjacent to the proposed facility? What are the impacts of the accidental discharge of hazardous or toxic chemicals at the site?

C. <u>WATER QUANTITY</u>

1. What will be the environmental effect of the cumulative loss of nine cubic feet per second (C.F.S.) of fresh water from the Sacramento-San Joaquin Delta? What mitigation measures are proposed to offset these effects (including the impacts identified in Chapter 7 of the DEIS)? Specifically, what effects will this cumulative loss have on the ability of state and federal water agencies to meet delta water quality criteria? Also, how will this loss affect the provision of water to other users elsewhere in California?

2. What <u>alternative sources</u> of water supply are available for Dow's use? What are the costs and environmental impacts of these alternatives, and how do they compare with diversion from the Sacramento River? Could treated waste water from the East/Central Contra Costa Waste Water Management Project supply the proposed Pittsburg expansion? What factors determined the selection of fresh water over these alternatives?

3. On what basis does Dow claim riparian rights?

D. <u>DOCKING FACILITIES</u>

1. What size tankers and barges will the docking facilities at Pittsburg and Collinsville accommodate? What kind of pilings would be available for the tugboats and steamboats that push the barges into the dock? How could the barges be tied off? How will barges be rotated into place?

2. What loading and offloading procedures and techniques will Dow follow?

3. How will offloading facilities deal with residual tanker contents? How will offloading facilities deal with the problem of successively offloading products with vastly different properties? How will Dow prevent the discharge of residual contents into the bay?

4. How long will offloading of typical barges require? Could the docks be in use continuously?

5. What is the status of the Summary Marine Spills Assessment Report (May 1976) prepared by Dow? Will it be incorporated into the EIS? Has it been approved by Solano County or Contra Costa County? Will the summary report be expanded?

6. The expansion of docking facilities in the bay may pose a public safety hazard from ships moving into the docks. How would Dow supervise the quality of performance of pilots moving ships into the docks?

E. <u>DREDGING OPERATIONS</u>

1. What is the expected effect of dredging at the Dow site on heavy metal concentrations in surface waters?

2. What is the capability of the dredging disposal site, and where will subsequent spoils be placed?

3. Where will the 250,000 cubic yards from maintenance dredging be disposed each five years?

4. The proposed modifications of deepwater-shipping channels may require dredging to much greater depths. How will such dredging affect the planned burial depths of the pipelines connecting the two Dow facilities? Will reburial be required? What operational and environmental problems may result?

F. <u>PROJECT ALTERNATIVES</u>

1. What are the reasons for selecting the Montezuma site rather than an alternative site adjacent to the existing Pittsburg plant (that is, U.S. Steel property)?

2. What other alternatives for the Dow project have been identified in addition to those mentioned in the draft Environmental Impact Statement (that is, Washington State, Avon, Pittsburg, and Los Angeles)?

3. Are there alternatives available that are not mentioned in the draft EIS that would be more acceptable from an air quality standpoint? From the standpoint of deepwater access? From the standpoint of land use and agricultural impact? Indicate the basis for evaluating these alternatives.

G. <u>AIR QUALITY</u>

1. What types of emissions are possible from plant malfunctions and accidents, and what are the probabilities of the occurrence of each?

2. What is the current level of pollutant emissions at the existing Pittsburg plant? What is the record air quality violations of this plant?

3. What background levels of air quality are predicted using methods approved by the Bay Area Pollution Control District, the Air Resources Board, and the Environmental Protection Agency?

4. What are the planned operations scheduled for the area marked "future" in the figure II-5, page II-31 of the DEIS? For the two areas shown to the right of plant site 4 in figure I-13, page I-19 of the DEIS but not labeled in figure II-5? Is any production of trichloroethylene or trichlorophenol planned for future development?

5. Dow has applied for an Authority to Construct from the Bay Area Air Pollution Control District for a styrene plant, 1 of the 13 plants of the proposed petrochemical complex. The APCD has denied this permit because emissions from this plant will interfere with the attainment and maintenance of ambient air quality standards for particulates, oxides, and hydrocarbons. Considering that the other 12 plants will produce additional emissions, how does Dow propose to meet these air quality requirements with the proposed facilities at the Collinsville and Pittsburg sites?

6. When natural gas is not available for use as a fuel, what are the emissions and air quality impacts resulting from the use of alternate fuels, including those with higher sulphur content?

7. Will the estimated air emissions include vinyl chloride? What are the possible effects on public health of vinyl chloride emissions and on the discharge of other organic chemicals into the air?

8. What is the nature and level of emissions expected from tanker unloading at the Dow plant? Are these included in the emission levels shown in the final EIR or the draft EIS?

H. <u>IMPACTS ON AGRICULTURE</u>

1. How will the proposed petrochemical facility affect agricultural lands in the Sacramento and San Joaquin Valleys?

2. What will be the effects of air pollution (for example, ethylene) on crops?

3. How are the Williamson Act cancellation and the rezoning of the site from agriculture consistent with the Solano County General Plan as it existed on the date of the cancellation? What was the basis for determining that these actions were consistent with the purposes of the Williamson Act and in the public interest?

4. What is the <u>net</u> profit or <u>net</u> loss in the value per acre of land for the site after the proposed industrialization?

I. <u>GEOLOGIC AND SEISMIC CONCERNS</u>

1. Will the plant, the storage tanks, the water storage dam, the pipelines, and the evaporation ponds be constructed to withstand the maximum credible seismic event

from all causative faults including a magnitude 6.5 on the Antioch fault? If not, what mitigating measures will provide positive assurances that there will be no effect on public safety and the environment?

2. If potential damages are not mitigable in the event of failure due to an earthquake, what will be the expected effects on public safety and the environment?

J. <u>IMPACTS ON FISH AND WILDLIFE</u>

1. What would be the net loss of wildlife habitat from construction and operation of the Dow petrochemical facility and expected satellite industries?

2. What are the magnitudes of potential wildlife losses from pipelines connecting the existing and proposed Dow facilities? From spills of toxic chemicals? From associated dredging activities in the bay?

3. What is the impact on wildlife of dredging operations in the San Francisco Bay? Would increased turbidity from dredging enter the Suisun Marsh? With what effect?

K. <u>ENERGY CONSUMPTION AND USE</u>

1. How will the location of the petrochemical facility in the San Francisco Bay Area affect the disposition of Alaskan crude oil along the West Coast? The current petroleum processing on the West Coast? The cost of petroleum products to West Coast consumers?

2. North Slope oil, one source of naphtha, will last for an estimated 15 years. What alternative sources of naphtha, the feedstock for the Dow facility, are available? How will the use of these future alternative sources allow Dow to produce plastic raw materials and still make a profit?

L. <u>ECONOMIC AND EMPLOYMENT IMPACTS</u>

1. Describe the costs of city government services expected to be directly attributable to the Dow project? (For example, school facilities, water supply facilities, wastewater facilities, police, and fire protection, etc.)

2. How much in local government costs for public services will the Dow facilities contribute? Who will bear the burden of such costs? How will the revenues generated by the facilities be distributed to the local jurisdictions (cities and counties)?

3. The draft EIS (Chapter IX-129) documents the number of new jobs resulting directly and indirectly from construction of Dow facilities. It provides economic "multipliers" of 1.72 and 1.85 for the Fairfield-Vacaville area and the Antioch-Pittsburg-Concord area, respectively, to quantify the induced employment from increased demand for goods and services. The draft EIS cites an analysis by the Stanford Research Institute (SRI) as the basis for these

"multipliers." Please provide a copy of the SRI analysis and any supporting data used in this analysis to allow an independent evaluation of the economic impacts.

M. <u>CUMULATIVE AND GROWTH-ASSOCIATED IMPACTS</u>

1. What are the potential cumulative impacts of Dow and the subsidiary industries (for example, those industries using Dow's products that are likely to site in the Bay Area) on both the county and the region?

2. What would be the cumulative impacts of such subsidiary industries on air quality? In particular, what would be the frequency and extent of air emissions from such industries (for example, a vinyl chloride polymerization plant)?

3. What is the cumulative effect of the proposed project and the subsidiary industries on the demand for fresh water in Solano County, the delta, and the Central Valley?

4. Where are the final markets for Dow products (plastic raw materials)? What are the exact locations of subsidiary industries in California that will manufacture Dow's products into consumer goods?

5. How will the Dow project and the subsidiary industries affect the likelihood of future growth and development in the Bay Area?

6. What interrelationships exist between the Dow project and the proposed modifications of the San Francisco, Stockton, and Sacramento Ship Channels? Would the Dow project encourage the deepening of the existing deepwater channel from 35 to 45 feet in the Collinsville area?

7. What effects of the Dow proposal could be mitigated by the incorporation of the Dow project in the proposed deepwater port facility at Collinsville? What effect would independent establishment of the Dow project have on support for a port facility with appropriate installations for the protection of water quality from spills?

8. How would infrastructure associated with the Dow project such as extensions and improvements of road and rail transportation, affect the growth of industry in the surrounding areas?

9. How will Solano County's cancellation of the Williamson Act contract and rezoning of the parcel from agriculture to general manufacturing affect the conversion of other agricultural lands in Solano County? How will this cancellation affect the conversion of agricultural lands elsewhere in the Sacramento-San Joaquin Delta?

11
Energy—
The Strip Mining of Coal

THE FIRST OF THE MANY

The problem of the conflict between demands for the maintenance or improvement of living standards and the needs of the environment has already come to a spectacular head in the world's demands for energy. Insofar as the development "environmental problem" is on the one hand the product of inevitably increasing calls on natural resources, and on the other a growing awareness of the importance of the environment, the aftermath of the artificially induced energy crisis that followed the Yom Kippur War of October 1974 has highlighted the kinds of choices we will have to make in the future with respect to all kinds of natural resources. The most critical relationships between energy consumption and reserves in various parts of the world are illustrated in Tables 11.1 and 11.3. Perhaps because it was unanticipated, the crisis encapsulated the running tide of events and compressed an emerging series of difficulties into a relatively brief span of time. How these questions are being handled demonstrates in a graphic way the reality of all resource conflicts.

This case was written by D. J. Davison, _The Environmental Factor_ (London: Associated Business Programs, 1978), pp. 101–28, adapted. Reprinted with permission.

WHEN THE PETROL PUMP RUNS DRY

While this is certainly not the place to become involved in a discussion of the rights and wrongs of the Yom Kippur War, we need to remind ourselves of one or two facts to put the oil crisis in perspective.

As most people will remember, the Arab nations decided to intervene by attempting to bring pressure on Israel through third parties. They thought that this would be helped by cutting off supplies of oil, especially to those nations that were thought to be sympathetic to or actively supporting Israel.

The Arab nations were convinced that such actions were necessary to bring about what they would regard as a satisfactory outcome of the war. They had appreciated the crucial nature of oil supplies to developed nations. In the event, their actions can be seen as having a profound effect on the attitudes of these countries to the problem of energy supplies. It was, as the Arabs had foreseen, a direct attack on the jugular vein of developed nations, which had lulled themselves into the belief that supplies of cheap oil would continue forever and when any attempt was made to cast doubt on this belief, the argument was dismissed as being the biased product of special interests. For example, although the National Coal Board had been pointing out throughout the 1960s that Britain was becoming increasingly vulnerable to any curtailment of its oil supplies, no serious consideration was given by governments to this viewpoint, and the proportion of the country's energy needs met by oil continued to increase. Only the fortuitous finding of oil in the North Sea has saved this country from irretrievable disaster.

To get some flavor of the official thinking of the time in Britain, it is worth looking at the White Paper on fuel policy, Cmnd 3438 published in 1967, which assumed the continuance of cheap oil supplies into the foreseeable future. It concluded, "On the evidence available, it seems likely that oil will remain competitive with coal, and that pressure to force up crude oil prices will be held in check by the danger of loss of markets" (paragraph no. 53).

The Arab oil embargo caused many rapid and agonizing reappraisals, not only at the government level, but down to the policies of individual companies. In practice, policy proved difficult to implement, because it is hard to keep a tight control over the ultimate destination of oil once aboard the tanker and off into the wide blue yonder. But it was effective enough to show the power of the weapon that the oil-producing nations had forged. Inevitably, once the immediate crisis was over, the oil producers decided that they should seek to take greater advantage of their new strength, in order to build up their economies to face the day when their own supplies dried up. In a very short space of time, therefore, the consuming countries found themselves presented with a fivefold increase in oil prices.

TABLE 11.1
World Energy Consumption, 1950-70
(million tons coal equivalent)

	1951-55 Average		1966-69 Average	
	Amount	Percentage	Amount	Percentage
Coal, peat, etc.	1,669.4	56.3	2,276.3	38.6
Oil	802.0	27.0	2,327.7	39.5
Natural gas	359.6	12.1	1,149.3	19.5
Other*	135.4	4.6	139.4	2.4
Total	2,966.4	100.0	5,892.7	100.0

*Hydroelectric and nuclear.
Source: The Wharton School, University of Pennsylvania, Materials Requirements in the United States and Abroad in the Year 2000, Washington, D.C., 1973.

TABLE 11.2
World Proven Solid Fuel Reserves, 1968
(million tons oil equivalent)

Country	Proven	Inferred	Total	Percentage Share
Western Europe	32,350	44,350	76,700	1.3
Poland	26,000	14,800	40,800	0.7
USSR (including Asian USSR)	166,000	3,575,000	3,741,000	63.6
South Africa	24,500	24,500	49,000	0.8
Other Africa	4,000	5,570	9,750	0.2
China	—	680,000	680,000	11.6
India	8,500	64,750	73,250	1.2
Other Asia	6,500	15,750	22,250	0.4
South America	95,000	990,000	1,085,000	18.5
Central and South America	2,500	21,950	24,450	0.4
Australasia	35,500	40,500	76,000	1.3
World Total	400,850	5,477,350	5,878,200	100.0

Source: Commodities Research Unit and National Coal Board estimates.

TABLE 11.3
World Proven Oil and Natural Gas Reserves, 1973

	Oil Reserves		Gas Reserves	
	Millions of Tons	Percentage Share	Millions of Tons Oil Equivalent	Percentage Share
Western Europe	2,115.0	2.5	4,735.0	9.4
Caribbean, South America	4,303.0	5.0	2,252.0	4.5
Middle East	47,622.0	55.8	10,193.0	20.4
Africa	9,153.0	10.7	4,629.0	9.2
Indonesia	1,428.0	1.7	370.4	0.7
Other Asia	355.0	0.4	1,147.0	2.3
Australia, New Zealand	343.0	0.4	1,300.0	2.6
North America	6,001.0	7.0	7,339.0	14.6
Soviet Union	10,880.0	12.8	17,410.0	34.8
China	2,720.0	3.2	493.0	1.0
Other Communist	408.0	0.5	232.0	0.5
World Total	85,388.0	100.0	50,144.0	100.0

Source: Oil and Gas Journal 71 (December 31, 1973).

SHOULD WE BUY BICYCLES?

Overnight, countries had to wake up to the fact that what had been cheap energy, the lifeblood of their economies, had vanished from the scene and that they had to face a world in which energy costs would be a heavy and rising part of the cost of living. Anyone who installed oil-fired central heating prior to October 1974 should not need convincing of the truth of this statement!

For a while, many commentators argued that this "unnatural" increase in the price of oil was merely a direct product of the Arab-Israel conflict and that, before long, it would fall back to a more realistic level.[1] The argument was that the consuming nations would reduce their demand for oil, and the producers would be left with a surplus. This would weaken their general resolve to maintain the higher price, the unity of OPEC would be broken, and prices would fall to a "normal level." In practice, it looks as though the best we can hope for is a mitigation of future price increases.

This approach that there would be an inevitable reduction in price ignored the fact that the pressure for substantial increases in oil prices did not come exclusively from the Arab nations. Leaders among the pressure groups for increased prices were Venezuela and Canada. There is now little doubt that, had Britain's North Sea oil reserves been a little nearer commercial exploitation, Britain itself would have been a fervent advocate of a major price increase to cover the costs of this development. As the energy crisis increases, Great Britain, with its massive reserves of coal and enormous finds of oil in the North Sea, has come to have a vested interest in a high oil price. The reason for this is simple. Where you find you have substantial physical reserves of natural resources vital to your economy, but where your own production costs are relatively high, then you have a strong incentive to do everything possible to raise the price to a level that will enable you to absorb your higher costs and make the overall operation profitable. A similar argument applied to Canada and to Venezuela. The net effect of the quintupling of oil prices almost overnight has been to make more reserves of oil available to the world, by making it increasingly economic to work them. Similarly, the world's more economic coal reserves have greatly increased. In the case of Great Britain, it is now sensible to embark on the "Plan for Coal"2 with its major investment in new and reconstructed mines to maintain, and eventually increase, capacity. In the United States attention is now focused on the "new" coal fields of the West. In Canada the price increases have resulted in the exploitation of the almost mythical reserves of the tar sands.

THINGS WILL NEVER BE THE SAME AGAIN

These events will, in their turn, have a profound effect on local environments in all these countries. Areas that were previously undisturbed by industry, such as the northeast coast of Scotland and the mid northwestern states of the United States, have now become boom areas, and their way of life has been transformed. Whether this is for better or for worse is, of course, the nub of the argument.

Because of this activity, and the fact that, until the mid-1970s the talk had been of oil surpluses, many assumed that the energy crisis was a politician's crisis, rather than a real one. There is a widespread belief that the crisis was always artificial. Some people have gone as far as to argue that it was partly manipulated by interested parties in order to boost the price of their products. This feeling was not helped when the major oil companies announced record profits in the years immediately following the major price increases.

This superficial analysis hardly bears examination. Whatever may be the truth of the short-term motivation behind the actions of energy producers or suppliers, the fact remains that even at these higher prices we are consuming our resources at a frighteningly fast rate. Total reserves of oil represent far fewer years of anticipated consumption than any other major energy resource (see Figure 11.1). Although new reserves will be found, it is probable that a major proportion of these will be found in the Middle East or in other countries that for one reason or another might be regarded as unreliable sources of supply (see Figure 11.2). The world will have to adjust from an era of a cheap and plentiful energy supply to one of scarce, dear energy. The result will be a consequential need to avoid unnecessary additions to production costs and to find acceptable ways of maximizing supplies.

FIGURE 11.1
1973 Crude Petroleum Production and
Petroleum Product Consumption for
Major Producing and Consuming Areas (MB/D)

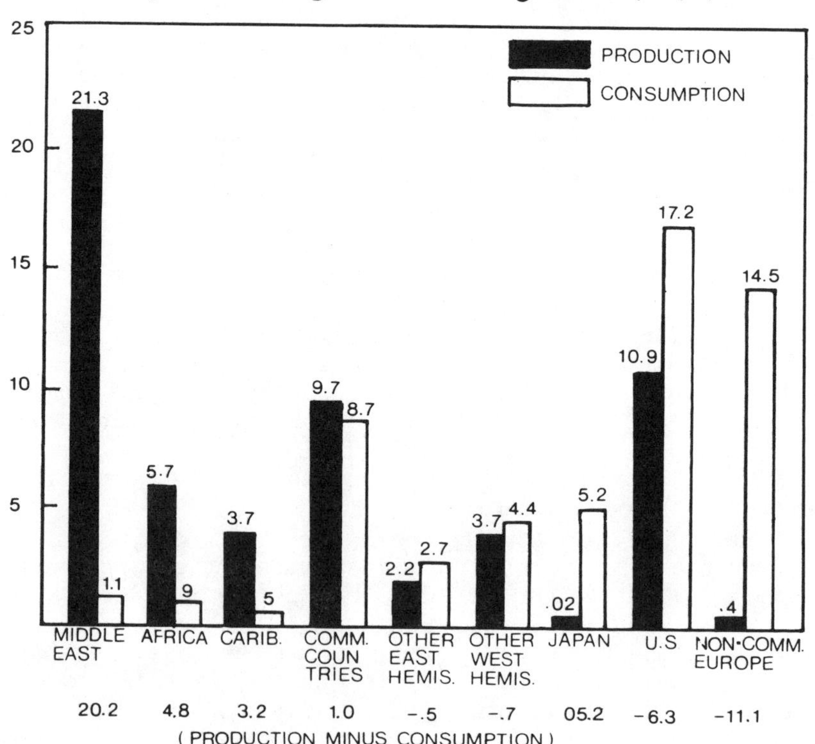

Source: Project Independence Report, November 1974, Federal Energy Administration.

FIGURE 11.2
1973 Crude Petroleum Reserves for Major Producing Areas

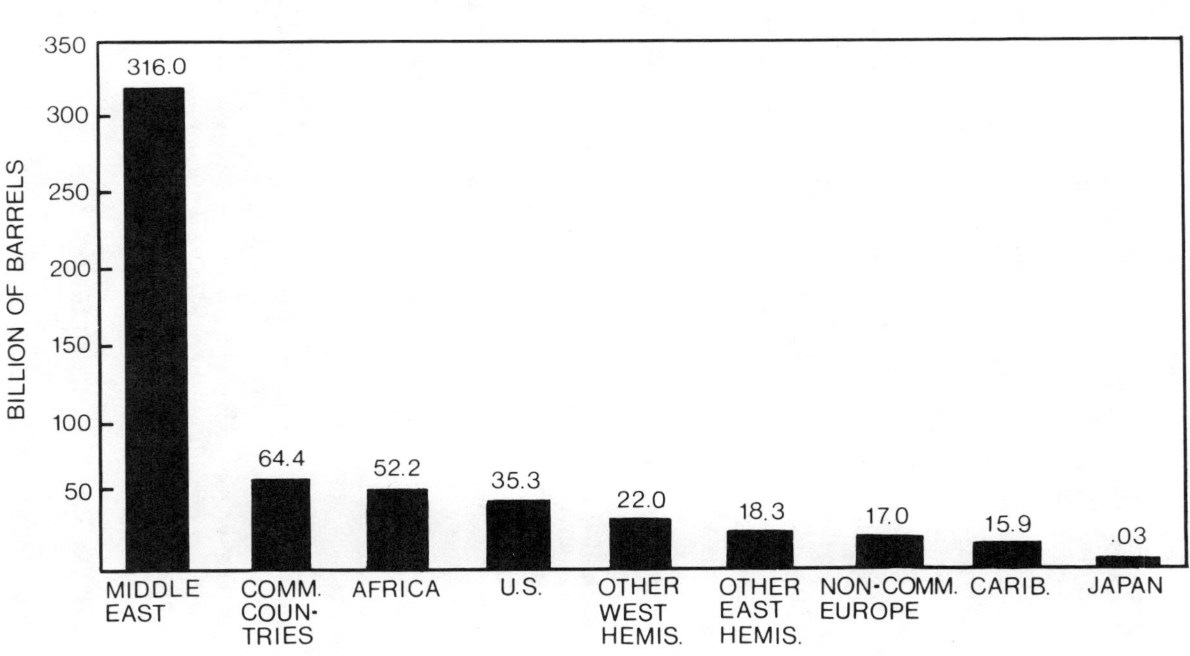

Source: Project Independence Report, November 1974, Federal Energy Administration

TO EACH HIS OWN

It is not surprising that faced with this situation countries have embarked on a scramble for energy self-sufficiency. This is likely in many areas of activity to lead to a confrontation with environmental interests. In this context the problems that arise are exemplified by those in the United States.

Until November 1973 the level of imports in the United States from Arab sources alone was some 3 billion barrels per day, or 70 percent of total demand. The effect of the short embargo was marked. Apart from the inconvenience caused by petrol shortages, the gross national product of the United States during the period dropped by some $10,000 million, and unemployment rose by some 50,000 workers.

Worried by these considerations, the U.S. government has embarked on "Project Independence." The professed aim of this program is to achieve self-sufficiency in energy within a period of ten years.3 This target seems far too ambitious. It has aroused expectations that probably were never likely to be fulfilled, and hope of making the target a reality has been effectively killed, since it was adopted at a time when federal and state governments were in the process of tightening the environmental standards for air, water, nuclear generation, and strip mining.

The _Project Independence Report_ considered three broad strategic options: an increase in domestic supplies of energy; conserving and managing energy demand; and establishing standby emergency programs.

What is significant is the speed at which the change came over the U.S. energy scene. Until 1950 the United States was self-sufficient in energy. The situation deteriorated rapidly in the following 25 years for three main reasons. First, coal production remained static. Second, crude oil production has been in a decline since 1970 and, last, natural gas consumption has been exceeding annual new sources since 1968. Thus, by 1973 the dependence of the United States on foreign oil had grown to 35 percent of domestic petroleum consumption. (It is interesting to note that the report comments that the strategic implications of oil imports were highlighted by the Arab-Israeli conflict, rather than created by them.)

DO YOU WANT TO SEE THE STRIP SHOW?

The _Project Independence Report_ sets out a strategy for increasing energy supply within the United States as a first and fundamental aim, although it also acknowledges that this raises major environmental problems, the main reason being that one of the quickest ways of increasing energy supply is to go for a major expansion in coal production. In terms of reserves, there was no problem: in 1974 coal production was running at some 600 million tons, whereas reserves were estimated as being more than 400 billion tons. Project Independence called for a doubling of coal production by 1985, but the immediate problem is that, given this period of time, most of this increase would have to come from surface or strip mining production. Over the years strip mining of coal in the United States has built up a bad reputation for its environmental record, derived from the method of work and the relatively scant attention that has been paid to the environmental problems it created.

In its simplest terms, strip mining consists of nothing more than removing the top soil, rock, and other strata in order to recover the mineral or fuel deposits below them. The problems arise in relation to what is done with the overburden (for example, the material that must be removed to get the mineral, both during and after working). There are many ways in which this simple-sounding process can be carried out, some of which have far more profound effects on the environment than others.

In the United States, a particular method of surface mining, known as contour mining, has caused considerable environmental damage. Contour mining consists of removing the overburden above the coal by starting where the coal outcrops and then proceeding along the hillside. Frequently the overburden is just cast down the hillside. The result is that a shelf, or bench, is formed on the hillside while, unless controlled or stabilized, the overburden cast down the hillside can cause severe erosion and landslides. The most notorious areas of this activity are in Appalachia, where some 20,000 miles of benches were created and, in some cases, completely isolated entire mountain tops. In Pennsylvania large areas of woodlands, which had helped to retard runoff, have been destroyed. Material washed from the overburden banks has seeped over adjoining downhill areas and choked streams. Effluent from the mine has formed in pools and become acid. Many areas spoiled by mining operations were abandoned, without any attempt at restoration. There is no doubt that environmental degradation caused by surface mining has become widespread and serious in some parts of the United States.

This is not the whole story, however. The problem has been appreciated for some time. In fact, the Indiana Coal Producers' Association was founded in 1919 to revegetate part of the banks spoiled by coal operations. The first strict mine legislation was introduced in West Virginia in 1939, and other states have subsequently passed their own regulations. These are of differing quality, but in recent years the number and severity of them have increased. At the time of writing, some 33 states have surface mining and mined land reclamation laws, and new regulations have been proposed by the Department of the Interior.

DO WE WANT A COVER UP?

For a variety of reasons, much of the strip mining in the United States was done without any thought being given to the end use for the land or the possibility, or practicability, of restoration. There are considerable areas of previously strip mined land in the United States that have not been in any way restored. It has often been argued that the cost of restoration would far exceed the worth of the land "created." This is to miss the point entirely. Landscape in this sense has no economic price, and the cost of restoration should be seen as the cost of working the area in the first place. This action on the part of some operators naturally caused considerable resentment, both in the community where they have operated and among environmental protection bodies and conservation societies.

When it was understood that, in order to double coal production in the United States in the ten-year period, it would be necessary to more than double the area of land to be strip mined, then it will be appreciated that considerable concern and opposition was aroused. Congress members were under severe pressure to prevent what the opponents of the extension of strip mining saw as despoilation of the country. The result was that much lobbying took place, and a great deal of effort was put into a bill aimed at controlling surface mining.

This took the form of an ongoing political struggle. Though the Surface Mining Control and Reclamation Act (SMCRA) was enacted in 1977, it was, in fact, the third attempt at such legislation. Previous versions had been vetoed by President Ford in 1974 and 1975.

Joseph Kalt and Mark Zupan have described the SMCRA as follows:

> The Surface Mining Control and Reclamation Act was signed into law by President Carter on August 3, 1977. SMCRA empowered the Department of the Interior to promulgate and enforce nationwide mining and reclamation regulations. The central thrust of the Act is to require the complete restoration of strip mined land to its pre-mining state upon the cessation of mine operations. Surface coal mines, as well as the surface operations of underground coal mines, must return utilized land to approximate original contour and productivity. Reclaimed land must be revegetated and stabilized so as to prevent soil erosion and damage to hydrologic systems. During

mining, mine operations and overburden disposal must be managed so as to prevent acid drainage, waterway sedimentation, and damage to neighboring property. To provide for the reclamation of already-stripped land, an Abandoned Mine Reclamation Fund is supported by a $.35 per ton tax on surface bituminous coal production, a $.15 per ton tax on underground bituminous coal production, and a $.10 per ton tax on lignite coal production.

In addition to direct regulation of the environmental impacts of strip mining, SMCRA addressed itself to the problems of property rights assignments in water, land, and recreational and aesthetic amenities. The Act prohibits surface mining in the National Park System, National Wildlife Refuge System, National System of Trails, the Wilderness Preservation System, and Custer National Forest in Wyoming. Surface mining is technically permitted (but effectively prohibited) in National Forests if there are no significant recreational, timber, economic, or other values that would be adversely affected. Prime farmlands cannot be strip mined unless the land can be returned to equivalent or higher agricultural yields. Alluvial valleys in the West cannot be mined if mining disrupts or precludes farming. Importantly, where surface rights and subsurface mineral rights are held by different parties, subsurface right holders (leasees) must obtain written consent from surface right holders before commencing strip mining if subsurface rights were originally federally owned. Where both surface and subsurface rights are privately owned, disputes are to be settled in accordance with state law. Finally, if state surface mine regulations can be shown to be at least as stringent as SMCRA, a state may elect to supercede the federal regulation.[4]

HAVE WE ANY CHOICE?

In its environmental assessment of the possible options open in the United States, the report on Project Independence stated that:

The United States does not have to make an absolute choice between energy development and a clean environment. These goals are not mutually exclusive, or their actions taken to develop energy would inevitably have environmental implications, and certain environmental standards would strongly affect energy growth. Environmental protection must be placed in perspective with other national goals, such as economic development, social welfare and energy security. To a large extent the energy and environmental decisions, made in the near future, will determine our future lifestyles.

To see how things might be done better, the United States has looked in the direction of Europe and, in particular, at West Germany and Great Britain. The experiences here have been different and the direct conflict facing the United States, so far, has been avoided.

OPENCAST MINING IN BRITAIN AND
WEST GERMANY: A PRACTICAL EXAMPLE

Of all the industrial activities that arouse the wrath of the environmentalists and conservationists, it is hard to think of one that causes as much of an outcry as that of strip mining. In many people's minds, strip mining has become synonymous with an attack on civilized living standards, the epitome of all that is wrong in the attitude of industry to the environment in which it lives.

That this attitude exists is hardly surprising. Strip mining, by definition, involves the removal of the immediate land overlying the mineral, and it is hard to think of anything more potentially destructive. The whole operation is seen in highly emotive terms as the rape of the countryside, the tearing apart of the natural landscape. These are all phrases that spring to the mind of even moderately well-informed conservationists or environmentalists.

The question is, therefore, why do people try to persist with opencast mining, and is it really ever defensible? In the terms that I have been describing, is it possible to imagine a compromise between the needs of the environment and the industrial operation itself?

In raising these questions, whether or not strip mining should be banned either in part or whole, the various issues that I have been discussing so far are brought into focus and, for this reason, the example of the way a compromise on opencast coal mining in Great Britain has been sought is worthy of detailed study. The lessons, both good and bad, have much to offer industry in general.

Opencast coal mining in Britain began in 1942. The date is significant, because it was in the middle of World War II, at a time when the German Atlantic blockade was proving very effective, and Great Britain's attempts to build up its armaments and fighting power were being gravely handicapped by lack of fuel. At that time, the only way in which additional volumes of fuel could be made available was from the coal-mining industry. The deep-mined industry was already producing as much as it could, and the situation was so desperate that workers were being put into the pits by the simple expediency of making work in the pits the equivalent of serving in the armed forces. A scheme was adopted whereby, under a process of ballot, men who were being enrolled for the armed services found themselves instead being drafted to a colliery to work underground.

Against this backdrop of national emergency a number of civil engineers in Great Britain suggested that there might be pockets of coal that could be produced by adopting the United States' method of stripping off the covering of the coal and simply digging it out. It was agreed that this should be done, U.S. expertise and some machinery were imported, and the whole operation got under way. It will be appreciated that the unity of purpose inspired by the war effort was such that arguments against producing the coal in this way, because of the effects on the landscape, were hardly likely to be given great weight. But it is significant that from the very beginning, the British government provided that all areas that were being opencasted should be restored to their previous use. This turned out to be a fundamental and well thought out decision. It meant that from the beginning the industry had to become accustomed to handling the restoration problems as well as those of production.

After the war ended the need for coal continued at a high level, but the immediate pressure of the "enemy at the gates" had receded and, not surprisingly, pressure to improve restoration techniques began to grow.

Although restoration had to be carried out during wartime, there was little insistence on getting the best possible standards. The immediate problem was to keep the coal production flowing, and there was a strong tendency to have plant and men transferred from restoration to further production sites as rapidly as possible. This was not an argument that could be used once the pressures for supplies lessened.

This did not happen in the immediate postwar period. Shortages of energy, in those days almost entirely coal, were seen as the fundamental problem holding back economic development. The then British foreign secretary, Ernest Bevin, said that the greatest help he could have for his foreign policy was a surplus of coal to export. Then, about 1957, the situation changed.

Helped by a well-mounted and well-conceived selling campaign and backed by heavy rebating, the oil companies made major inroads into the market, which had traditionally been supplied by the coal industry. The demand for coal dropped very sharply, and the long-term investments that had been made in the coal industry in the 1950s, with the object of increasing annual coal production in Great Britain by up to 240 million tons a year, began to appear ill-conceived. As demand dropped, pressure was brought on the coal industry to reduce, if not eliminate, the production of opencast coal. By this time, a major commercial problem was that the opencast coal production was far more economic and, as such, made a major contribution to the coal industry's efforts to fight oil competition. In those circumstances, the industry was having to deprive itself of its most economic source of production, at a time when it needed the maximum production to keep its average prices down and so compete with its rivals.

A further difficulty was that opencast production happened to produce some very high quality coals that were not readily available in deep mines, and it was essential that production of these coals should be maintained.

In 1957 the government decided that the whole issue of opencast mining should be dealt with under a special planning law. They therefore introduced the Opencast Coal Act, which laid down in detail the ways in which the National Coal Board could attempt to get approval for the working of opencast coal sites. Specific provision was made to enable any local objectors who had a direct interest in the operation to make their views known to the authorities, and if they maintained their objections to proposals for working any particular site, then the minister in charge of the coal industry had to call a public inquiry under an independent inspector to assess the merits of the National Coal Board's case for working the site, together with the arguments against such working put forward by the objectors (see Appendix 11.3). Following the inquiry, the inspector would then submit a report and recommendations to the minister.

In such a situation it was essential (in fact, it was provided for in the Opencast Coal Act) that a detailed description of the proposed restoration be provided. Over the years, detailed practices have been built up in applying for sites, and it is worthwhile considering them in detail.

When members of the National Coal Board wish to work a coal deposit by opencast methods, they first of all drill the proposed area to see whether they have an economic and workable site. If this is the case, they then call a site meeting with all the interested parties: the landowners, the tenants, their agents, the Ministry of Agriculture, and local authorities. This meeting is held on the site and its purpose is twofold. First, it enables the National Coal Board to explain to the people most directly concerned what the effect would be of the proposals if adopted. Second, it enables the people on the receiving end to make their comments and to point out difficulties or objections that would arise if work proceeds.

If representatives of the National Coal Board wish to go ahead, they have to make formal application to the secretary of state for energy under the terms of the Opencast Coal Act of 1957.

Britain is one of the most densely populated countries in the world. The task of trying to work surface mining with due regard to the environment is made doubly difficult because it inevitably affects far more people, both directly and indirectly, than would be the case in a more sparsely populated country. In Britain the technique used is most probably area strip mining, in which a series of parallel cuts are made, with the overburn from each cut being deposited in the void created by the previous cut. In some countries the final cuts are left open, but in Britain they are always filled with the overburden from the first cut.

Objections to opencast coal mining in Britain have always been made on environmental grounds. They cover two important, but distinct, aspects:

- The disturbance to the environment and to the people living in the area, which takes place during the working of the site;
- The danger of permanent changes in the landscape and damage to the land itself.

It is interesting to note how the weight of objections has moved from the second category to the first. This is basically because, in Britain, opencast mining has always been under centralized control. Originally under the control of the Ministry of Works, later the Ministry of Fuel and Power, final responsibility was given to one central body in 1952 — the National Coal Board. But from the very beginning complete restoration of a site has always been mandatory. The fact that all major opencast work in Britain is under the control of a central body is a great advantage in terms of restoration. It means that the National Coal Board does its utmost to ensure that standards of restoration are high throughout its activity. Any signs of omission or commission on a site in one part of the country are quite likely to be quoted against the National Coal Board by organizations or industries trying to prevent it being allowed to operate in another part of the country. The Opencast Executive has built up a worldwide reputation for the quality of the restoration carried out on opencast sites. The way in which this has been done has been the subject of much study from abroad, particularly the United States, faced as it is with the current concern to protect the environment while getting the additional coal needed from surface mining.

Because opencast mining in Britain has been under unified control, it has been possible to incorporate the cost of restoration as a "prime cost" in planning the feasibility of any particular operation, thus reducing the need to cut corners or to make economies in cost at the expense of the restoration. This is of the utmost importance. As it is the aim of the Opencast Executive to build up production on a long-term basis, it is clearly essential that it do nothing that could tarnish its reputation or make further applications to the sites more difficult to obtain. This, in itself, provides a strong degree of self-policing and self-control.

As in West Germany, restoration is planned when the site is conceived and, frequently, it is found possible to provide something new in the restored land area that meets a social or economic need. For example, it is quite possible to create a country park, a recreational area, or a golf course as part of the restoration, if this is what the local community and the landowners want. There is therefore no reason why the landscape should be affected in the long term, although it is true that the landscape will be changed; it is not possible to replace a wood or a hedge overnight. The crucial point here is to make sure they are replaced in the long term, if this is what people desire. People may be making some sacrifices in relation to the landscape as they have always known it, but these changes need not necessarily affect the succeeding generations, who will be faced with a different but, nevertheless, totally acceptable landscape.

An increasing amount of opposition to opencast sites is based on the disturbance that is caused during the working of the area. This is a very difficult problem. Working sites by opencast methods near urban areas does result in a number of disturbances — albeit mainly of a temporary nature — to the local inhabitants. The point is that the effects can be mitigated, if not eliminated, and an increasing amount of work is being done to tighten up on the protection of amenities during site working, while the costs of this must be seen as an essential part of the operation. New ways to control operations, in order to minimize disturbance, are thus constantly being investigated and brought into operation.

As many of these problems as possible are discussed and thrashed out, both within the Opencast Executive and with the planning authorities concerned, before the application on site takes place. Following authorization on the site, the National Coal Board offers to set up a liaison committee with the local residents and their representatives, to keep a careful watch on the progress of the site and to discuss any worries or concerns that local residents may have. It is obviously of the utmost importance to do everything possible to remove the reasons for complaints that may arise.

The opencast operation in Britain has worked and restored well over 100,000 acres of land, the vast majority of which is back in full-scale agricultural production. The operation has produced much needed coal (a high proportion of the coal produced from opencast methods in Britain is of a high quality and in short supply from the deep mines). It has thus made a major contribution to the economy of the country while at the same time, through intelligent land use and not leaving behind the moonscapes seen in parts of the United States, has restored Britain's rolling countryside. The operation is still far from perfect, but it does represent a major step forward in reconciling the twin objectives of economic prosperity and concern for the environment.

THE WEST GERMAN EXPERIENCE

West Germany has massive reserves of brown coal (lignite), amounting to some estimated 60,000 million tons. Since lignite provides a third of all power generated in West German thermal electric power stations, the resource is of crucial importance to the economy of the country. This vital role has been recognized by the West German government, and a tremendous modernization program has been undertaken. Since the end of World War II, more than a billion dollars have been invested in the industry, which has been fully consolidated. Many shallow surface mines, formerly common in the Rhineland, have been replaced by larger and more efficient open pit operations. This is demonstrated by the fact that, whereas the number of active mines in the Rhineland has decreased over the last 25 years from 23 to 6, the annual production of brown coal has increased from 64 million to 100 million tons.

The main companies have merged to form the present day Rheinische Braunkohlen Werke AG. The size of the operation and its unity have been important factors in allowing it to institute enlightened land reclamation practices. The discarded spoil material is filled back into the mined-out pits and then levelled off. The land is returned to agriculture, forests are planted, and new lakes created. It has become customary to follow the coal, even to the extent of moving villages that lie in the way, and new towns have been designed and built for displaced people. The basic resettlement costs are borne by the mining company, with local and state governments providing supplementary funds to pay for the incremental costs of better schools and other community services.

This comprehensive approach has shown how integrated the solution to the problem needs to be. By accepting the need for the result, in this case brown coal, and meticulously planning for it in advance, it has been possible to minimize the environmental effects and, in many cases, create something better than what existed before. This tremendous achievement shows what can be done if intelligence is applied to solving the problems.

LESSONS TO BE LEARNED

The examples above show how it is possible to answer apparently irreconcilable differences between the needs of the economy and the interests of the environment. I am not suggesting that the environmentalists have been totally satisfied with the solutions. Neither, for that matter, have the people involved in the exploitation of the mines. In reaching agreement on those areas that can be worked in Britain, some areas of coal have been excluded, at high cost, for environmental reasons. (Where these decisions have been made as the result of the recommendations of an inspector at a public enquiry, the cost of the environmental protection may not be known, because inspectors' recommendations to pull back a boundary for a few hundred feet may remove the most economical part of the coal area and result in economic nonsense.) Nevertheless, compromises have proved to be possible.

The West German experience is perhaps the best example, in that it shows what can be achieved if, at the beginning, the overall long-term objectives are accepted, and the concentration from then on is aimed at meeting the very proper environmental concerns.

It will be seen that in these examples a tremendous amount of work and effort has to be made in planning the site from scratch, to minimize the environmental impact during the period of working and maximize the quality of the restoration once the mineral has been extracted. To get this right does involve a major application of money and resources. Experience has shown that an attempt to take cheap short cuts is always the most expensive in the long run.

It should also be noted that in the planning and during the period of operation it has been found essential, as well as worthwhile, to involve the local inhabitants and planning authorities to the maximum possible degree. Problems are not necessarily solved through such means, and it would be foolish to believe that this might be the case, but we must try to reach a real appreciation of each other's aims and objectives and see what might be done to make them coincide a little more closely.

USE SOMETHING ELSE

One argument often put forward in relation to the strip mining of coal is that alternative fuels should be used instead, the assumption being that these must be somehow less inherently destructive of the environment. The U.S. Federal Energy Administration's Report did not take such a simple way out. It suggested that, whatever happened, there would have to be what it called "major environmental tradeoffs." In terms of the United States, it defined these as:

1. New versus existing areas of production. This is a tradeoff because most of the major coal reserves are in the areas where coal production has not expanded on any considerable scale. Therefore, there is the problem of accustoming new areas to the environmental impact of coal.
2. Nuclear power versus fossil fuels. Whereas nuclear power is undoubtedly a clean operation and, on the face of it, has major environmental advantages, its potential, even if not probable, environmental drawbacks are severe indeed. There are major problems of waste disposal: it is becoming increasingly unacceptable to think of dumping waste in "concrete overcoats" to the depths of the sea, because no one dare envisage the effect of such waste eventually seeping into the sea and subsequently into the human habitat. The potential seriousness of any accident hardly needs elaboration, and there is a further critical complication in that it now seems clear the countries can easily develop nuclear energy into atomic weaponry. This poses a major threat to the stability of the world and, as such, is a fundamental environmental objection to further massive nuclear expansion.
3. Location of facilities. The difficulty is in deciding whether to site the production capacity near the source of supply or near the source of demand. If near the source of demand, the environmental disadvantages associated with the form of energy being used will be existing side by side with large centers of population. If, on the other hand, they are sited near to the source of production, then there is the problem of transporting such energy to the centers of demand. This can lead to requirements for major electricity grids or pipelines, with all that this means in terms of environmental disturbance.
4. Renewable versus nonrenewable resources. How far should we concentrate on the rapid use of nonrenewable resources, particularly oil, at the expense of more renewable ones, such as wind and water?
5. Degrees of environmental damage. Some pollution can be rectified, and we have already discussed the rectification of major environmental upheavals caused by strip mining. Other types of pollution are irreversible — particularly nuclear.

All these tradeoffs have to be taken into consideration when deciding what is in the overall interest of a community in terms of energy policy. In practice, the arguments tend to be conducted at a very localized level indeed; for example, it is the individual directly affected who will raise the strongest objection. It is right that this personal aspect should be given sympathetic attention and, where appropriate, provision be made to alleviate the disturbance. The people who have to accept a worsening of their own environment should be compensated. It is not right, however, that such considerations should necessarily always be the deciding factor in how the policy is decided. It is all too easy to wish the problem from your own doorstep onto somebody else's.

We must, in the example of energy, as with all scarce natural resources, maximize the use of those categories that have the least effect on the environment. But we have to remember that all of them, to some extent, have some effect — we cannot eliminate, but only minimize, the problem. Even hydroelectric plants affect land use and river ecology, although these would normally be regarded as minor disturbances. The issue we have to face is not whether the environment will be disturbed, but in what way will it be the least disturbed and what can be done to alleviate the difficulties caused to individuals by the disturbance. We cannot live without energy; every effort must be made to maximize our production of energy. The world economy depends upon having sufficient energy to keep it moving. In such an important area, it is essential that all concerned do everything possible to fulfill the essential needs of the community with the minimum impact on the environment.

APPENDIX 11.1

Summary of the Provisions of the United Kingdom Opencast Coal Act of 1957

PROSPECTING

Prospecting is carried out under the terms of the Opencast Coast Act and of the General Development Order. The National Coal Board may carry out prospecting after the service of 42 days' notice on local authorities and after having obtained the consent of landowners and occupiers. If consent is not obtainable, the Board may compulsorily enter land after obtaining a direction from the responsible Minister (at present, the Secretary of State for Trade and Industry). Compensation is payable for any damage or disturbance caused during prospecting.

SITE WORKING

No site may be worked by the National Coal Board without the grant of an authorization by the Secretary of State for Trade and Industry.

When preparing working proposals, the National Coal Board is required by the Opencast Coal Act to take into account any effects its proposals may have on the natural beauty of the countryside; flora, fauna, buildings of historical or architectural interest, and any other relevant features must be given due consideration.

Before application for authorization to work a site is made, the National Coal Board must advertise its intention in the press, and it must serve notice on all local authorities and statutory undertakers concerned and on all individuals with an interest in the land. A period of 28 days is allowed for objections to be made. If objections raised by bodies or individuals who have an interest in the land cannot be resolved, the Secretary of State for Trade and Industry must order a public inquiry to be held. The secretary may also order a public inquiry at his or her own discretion even if no objections are made by the above parties.

The application submitted by the Board must consist of:

- Map showing the land that it will require to occupy and the parts of that land on which coal will be worked by opencast operations.
- Description of the operations to be carried out on the land.
- Description of the restoration operations.

- Statement of the Board's case for working the site.
- The application must be made available for public inspection.

If authorization is granted, the Board must advertise the fact in the press, and it must serve notice to this effect on each of the interested parties. The authorization must be made available for public inspection.

ENVIRONMENTAL ASPECTS OF OPENCAST COAL WORKING IN THE UNITED KINGDOM

1. Restoration code of practice

   a. Before working commences, topsoil (to a depth of 12 inches if available) and subsoil (to a depth of 24 inches if available) must be separately stripped from the site and stored in separate mounds. After working, the soils must be replaced on a graded overburden that is free of rocks, shale, and blue clay (which might impede a plough) to a depth of three feet.

   b. After working and the grading of the site and replacing subsoil and topsoil, the land is managed for five years on the Board's behalf by the Ministry of Agriculture. During this time, fences, hedges, ditches, farm roads, and other farm fixtures are reestablished and permanent underdrainage installed. Trees are planted in hedgerows, shelterbelts, and woodlands, and the land undergoes intensive agricultural management and treatment.

   c. Provision is also made for the land to be restored to forestry. In this case, the land is management for five years by the Forestry Commission, after being regraded to the contours required for planting.

2. Environment protection during site working
   Measures taken vary according to individual site conditions but generally include the following:

   a. Mounds of subsoil, topsoil, and overburden are sited so as to screen the site from the surrounding neighborhood and to act as baffles against noise and dust. They are gassed to improve their appearance.

   b. Blasting is limited to specific hours of the day.

   c. Wheel-washing bays are provided to prevent lorries from depositing mud on public roads.

   d. Site roads are watered in dry weather to reduce the incidence of dust.

e. The use of electrical machinery is specified wherever possible to reduce noise.

f. The diversion of streams and watercourses crossing the site and the construction of settlement lagoons to reduce the possibility of sediments leaving the site.

The Board will detail proposed environmental protection measures in the application for authorization, and the authorization will contain conditions enforcing these measures and any others that the Secretary of State for Trade and Industry deems desirable.

APPENDIX 11.2

United States Federal Energy Administration "Project Independence"6

The preceding chapter has made some reference to this report. It is a most comprehensive document and is essential reading for anyone who wishes to get an understanding of the complexity of the choices facing society. The details will be different for each country, but the principles and lessons of the analysis will remain equally valid. The following brief précis gives a little more background than could be contained in the chapter.

ALTERNATIVE ENERGY STRATEGIES

1. Accelerating domestic supply
The report concludes that this action could be inhibited by key constraints:

   a. Shortages of materials, equipment, and labor.
   b. Availability of drilling rigs.
   c. Financial and environmental control problems in the utility and railroad industries could hamper their ability to purchase convenient facilities and equipment.
   d. Water availability will be a problem in certain regions by 1985.
   e. Accelerating nuclear power plant construction does not have much effect on the reduction of imports in general. It replaces new coal-fired power plants.
   f. Accelerating synthetic fuel production would require by-passing key research steps and may not be cost effective or practical by 1985.

2. Energy conservation and demand management
Energy conservation actions can reduce demand growth to about 2 percent per year.
Actions can be taken that result in switching from petroleum and natural gas consumption to coal or coal-fired electric power. However, increased coal use in the pre-1985 period, by conventional building of coal-fired power stations, must be weighed against the possibility of increasing coal use by liquefaction and gasification in the post-1985 period.
The potential for coal development is virtually unlimited under accelerated conditions if no equipment, personnel, or demand constraints are assumed. Coal production could be over 2 billion tons per year in 1985 under these assumptions, although demand

limitations are likely to keep production to about 1 billion tons in 1985.

CRUDE OIL

The first fears of "running out of oil" were expressed in the early 1920s, and U.S. companies were urged by the government to develop oil production abroad to augment domestic supplies. In the 1930s the depression caused a break in demand and, with the subsequent development of the East Texas Field, the problem became one of containing the surplus oil production. As a result of these circumstances, oil production was concentrated in large vertically integrated companies, and state bodies became the regulators and conservers of crude oil production. State agencies began to control well spacing, restricting production to maximum efficient rates to prevent reservoir damage, and rating well production on the basis of market demand.

At the close of World War II, capacity was barely sufficient to meet market demand. By the mid-1950s, spurred by strong demand and rising prices, these lags were overcome. But oil reserves and the capacity to produce the required surplus stocks began to decline.

Production peaked in 1970, reserves having fallen each year since 1966, and drilling effort has only recently reversed its long-term downward trend.

Foreign oil became available at costs far below those of the United States' domestic production. Therefore major international oil companies expanded production in foreign areas. Federal government, concerned over the national security aspects, encouraged voluntary import restrictions in 1955 and 1957. In 1959 President Eisenhower invoked the national security provision of the Trade Agreement Extension Act to establish mandatory oil import quotas. Nevertheless, by 1970 the dependence of the United States on foreign oil sources had grown to 26 percent.

On April 18, 1973, the president suspended the Mandatory Oil Import Control Program, replacing it with a system of license fees that escalate with time. The License Fee Program is designed to support the long-term restoration and domestic capacity, while providing for the short-term need for imports.

In 1969 a major oil spill in the Santa Barbara Channel, and another on the Gulf Coast, directed attention to the environmental risks of offshore production. As a result, the Department of the Interior suspended the leasing of Pacific Continental Shelf acreage, pending the development of operating procedure and regulations to minimize the potential for future significant environmental damage.

Future supplies of oil will be determined by four fundamental factors:

- The amount of oil resources remaining to be found.
- Success in finding the remaining supply.
- Ability to recover what is found.
- The costs of the necessary exploration and production efforts.

The Federal Energy Administration found that:

The cost of the long lean times required to bring new petroleum fields into production is an important factor. Domestic production of crude and natural gas liquids will continue to decline for a few years regardless of higher prices or policies designed to encourage exploration. The major new source of oil production is Alaska. It is expected to provide between 3 and 5 million barrels per day. By 1985 Alaska could produce up to a quarter of United States oil, although, at present, it accounts for less than 2 percent.

The federal government controls about 40 percent of the remaining producible oil. How much of it will remain available for exploration and development depends upon consideration of environmental and ownership questions. The terms under which the government lands are made available affect the availability of capital, the rate at which these areas are explored and produced, and the proportion of oil in the place ultimately recovered.

Oil extraction, manufacturing, and distribution processes affect the quality of the environment. Oil spills can affect the marine environment, as well as creating aesthetic problems. Development of petroleum production has social and economic implications, especially in frontier areas. The Alaskan North Slope, with its fragile ecology and unpopulated areas, presents a particular series of problems. Its abundance of resources suggests that an extraordinary effort is needed to minimize environmental impact.

NATURAL GAS

The first natural gas well was put into production in 1821. Large discoveries took place in association with the development of the oil industry. The first large-scale use of natural gas was in the manufacture of steel and glass, in plants located in Pittsburgh. Initially, its use was confined to areas near gas or oil fields, but the development of long-distance gas transmission systems in the 1930s broadened its market. Immediately after the war, the availability of abundant supplies and improved quality enabled the gas utility industry to expand rapidly and widely. Marketing gas production increased from 4 trillion cubic feet (t.c.f.) in 1946 to 8 t.c.f. by 1952 and continued to grow at 6.5 percent in the 1950s and 1960s. It now represents about a third of the total energy consumed by the nation, including almost half of the nontransportation uses — and about twice that supplied by either oil or coal. One-half of the gas used is for residential and commercial purposes, one-sixth for the generation of electricity, and one-third for industrial uses.

In the 1970s the demand for gas has exceeded its supply. The Federal Power Commission has set priorities on gas use.

The Natural Gas Act of 1938 gave the Federal Power Commission authority to regulate interstate pipelines and natural gas imports and exports. In the Phillips Petroleum case in 1974, the United States Supreme Court held that a firm that produces and compresses gas and sells it to a pipeline company is a natural gas company. As a result, the Federal Power Commission began regulating the well head prices at which gas is sold in interstate commerce.

The commission found that natural gas will continue to decline in production at regulated price, until the 1980s. A sharp real increase in price could improve supply, but this will be dependent upon oil prices. In the meantime, consumption of natural gas is running at two or three times the rate of proving new resources.

COAL

Since 1950 the declining use of coal in the U.S. energy structure has been accelerated by government actions (see Figure 11.3). The development of nuclear electric power reduced the need for coal in generating electricity. The elimination in 1966 of world import quotas for residual oil on the East Coast resulted in many large coal users converting to cheaper and more convenient foreign oil. The implementation of the Clean Air Act during the 1970s has created significant uncertainties as to how much coal will be permitted to be burnt.

Coal reserves are estimated as being more than 400 billion tons, and more than half of them are located east of the Mississippi. Whereas nearly all of the coal reserves in the East are privately owned, most of the western coal reserves are owned by the federal government. Although 60 percent of the nation's coal reserves contain not more than 1 percent of sulphur, and most of this is in the West, a far smaller proportion of reserves can meet the sulphur dioxide performance standard for large boilers (for example, 1.2 lb of SO_2 per million btu's) established by the U.S. Environmental Protection Agency.

FIGURE 11.3
Coal's Declining Share of Total U.S. Energy Consumption

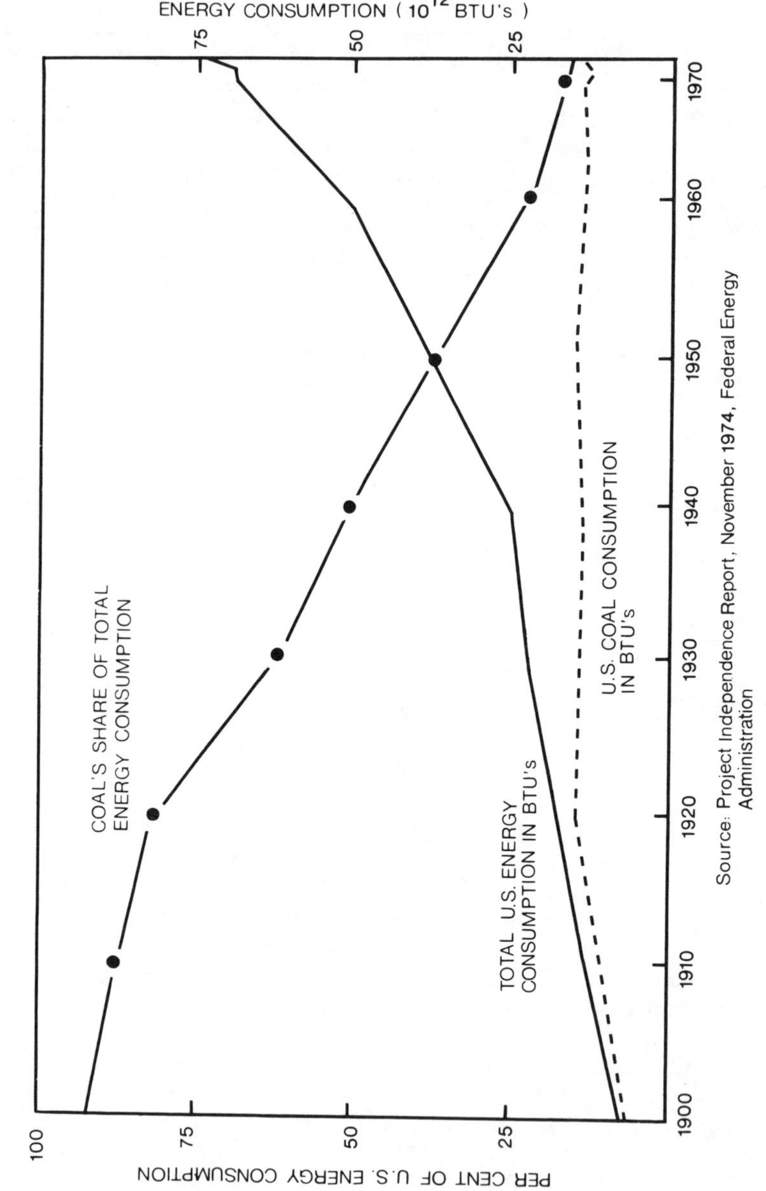

Source: Project Independence Report, November 1974, Federal Energy Administration

Coal production has not increased as fast as it could have because of the reluctance of owners to invest the major capital necessary to open up new mines. The capital has to be recovered over 20 to 25 years, and this level of markets had not been foreseen in the recent past. The future of coal has been clouded by uncertainties over strip-mining legislation. Western Coal Lands Leasing Policy, Clean Air implementation, oil import policy, natural gas pricing policy, and electricity demand forecast and nuclear capacity forecast.

The crucial factor here is whether the current emission regulations of power stations are enforced.

NUCLEAR FUELS

Earlier nuclear fuel production operations were sponsored by the U.S. government, with some private involvement. However, after the enactment of the Atomic Energy Act of 1954, private initiatives occurred in all phases of fuel production, with the exception of enrichment and permanent disposal of high-level radioactive waste, and have a major role in the development of most nuclear fuels. The federal government remains the sole supplier of enrichment services. In order to meet the projected accelerating nuclear generating plant schedule, nuclear fuel production and uranium enrichment would have to more than double between 1980 and 1985. Constraints are:

- Limited amount of uranium resources.
- The mining and milling capacity for uranium.
- The capacity for enriching uranium.
- The reprocessing capacity for spent fuel.
- Uncertainties about the schedule for nuclear generating capacity coming on stream.

The relatively low price of uranium has limited the exploration efforts, and the uncertain role of nuclear power in electric power generation has had a major limiting effect on development. (More recently, environmental concerns have come to the fore.)

Recovering usable uranium by reprocessing "spent" nuclear fuel could reduce new uranium requirements by about 15 percent and enrichment requirements by about 20 percent.

Public acceptance of nuclear power is an important factor in overcoming the current problems constraining the use of nuclear power and the exploration and mining of uranium.

SHALE OIL

Commercial production of liquid fuels from oil shale began in France in 1838. The Scottish oil shale industry started in 1850 and lasted until the 1950s, when production ceased due to the availability of lower-cost substitute fuels.

The federal government owns 72 percent of oil shale lands in the United States, and although there is a potential for major development of up to 200,000–300,000 barrels per day, the development would affect the environment. It is possible for levels to be expanded to over a million barrels per day by 1985, but this will only be considered if the price of oil remains high.

SYNTHETIC FUELS

The economic production of low btu fuel gas is dependent upon the development of new technology processes. Commercial production is expected to commence in the 1980s. At costs of $2 or more per million btu's in 1974, it was regarded as uncompetitive with natural gas. The decision is whether to deploy the existing technologies rapidly or wait for more efficient technologies.

Reliance on imports has generally positive domestic environmental effects, since many of the environmental impacts occur outside the consuming country.

However, adverse environmental effects from conventional energy development can be considerably mitigated through abatement measures such as surface mine reclamation, oil spill prevention technology, and emergency reactor core cooling systems.

APPENDIX 11.3

A Note on the National Coal Board

Readers in the United States may assume that the National Coal Board (NCB) is a department of British national government and thus subject to special conditions with regard to the environment that do not pertain to private industry. In fact, the conditions that govern the board's environmental role are no more stringent than the environmental constraints imposed on private industry operating in other realms of enterprise.

The NCB is a public corporation, whose stock is owned by the British government. Its responsibility is to manage the production and free market sale of coal at a profit. History has shown that NCB operates very much in the mold of a private company, although it has been subject over the years to some pressure from the government to effect labor settlements that were politically popular at the time.

There is, however, ample evidence that the NCB has operated with considerable independence in the management of its affairs, and that its interaction with other government agencies is much the same as that of private companies. In environmental matters, the NCB does not receive special favors or suffer special responsibilities. In short, its operations are typical of those that can be expected of private British industry, and it is appropriate to consider its environmental role as representative of British industry in general.

NOTES

1. See the editorials in the _Economist_ of the time. The _Economist_ must be one of the best written periodicals on business and public affairs in the world today, but it seems at times to have a touchingly naive faith in the ability of a supply and demand curve to solve the most profound of humanity's problems.

2. The policy for coal in Britain was considered by a tripartite body representing the National Coal Board, the government, and the mining unions. The findings of this group were set forth in the _Interim and Final Reports of the Coal Industry Examination_, published by the Department of Energy in 1974. These reports advanced the guidelines for the industry to follow in the next decade.

3. This theme was taken up by President Carter in his attempts to encourage energy conservation and to secure replacement prices for all types of consumption.

4. Joseph P. Kalt and Mark A. Zupan, "Coal Strip Mining Regulation and the Economics of Politics," no. 885, Discussion Paper Series (Cambridge, Mass.: Harvard Institute of Economic Research).

5. See first session of the Committee on Interior and Insular Affairs (Ninety-fourth Congress) on The President's Veto of H.R. 25, June 3, 1975.

6. In October 1983 the Reagan administration announced that it had formally abandoned the goal of energy independence contained in Project Independence, with the assertion that the United States would for the foreseeable future continue some dependence on Middle East oil. The project remains, however, as the most comprehensive statement of U.S. energy policy ever promulgated. The studies that led to the policy statement were used by Congress in the legislation of energy policy over many years, and the conclusions reached continue to animate U.S. energy policy. While the goal of energy independence was ephemeral, the concept provided, and continues to provide, fundamental guidance for federal action.

About the Author

C. WESLEY MORSE is a professor of management in the School of Business Administration, California State University, Long Beach. He was previously chief executive officer of Canfield Steel Corporation, now a subsidiary of Wheeling Pittsburgh Steel Company, and also headed his own firm of management consultants. He has been a member of the board of directors of a number of industrial companies.

Professor Morse received the B.S. degree in engineering from the University of California, Berkeley, and the Ph.D. in management from UCLA. His articles have appeared in the _California Management Review_ and other scholarly and business journals. He has lectured widely in the United States and Europe. He resides in Long Beach, California and spends several months of each year doing research and writing in countries of the European Community.